PROCEDURES
IN
FAMILY
THERAPY

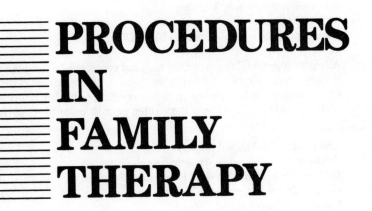

PROCEDURES IN FAMILY THERAPY

Gregory W. Brock
University of Kentucky

Charles P. Barnard
University of Wisconsin-Stout

With a Foreword by
Carl Whitaker, M.D.

ALLYN AND BACON, INC.
Boston   London   Sydney   Toronto

Series Editor: John-Paul Lenney
Production Coordinator: Annette Joseph
Editorial-Production Service: Publication Services
Cover Administrator: Linda K. Dickinson
Cover Designer: Christy Rosso
Manufacturing Buyer: Bill Alberti

Library of Congress Cataloging-in-Publication Data

Brock, Gregory, W., 1946–
   Procedures in family therapy.

   Bibliography: p.
   Includes index.
   1. Family psychotherapy. I. Barnard, Charles P. II. Title. [DNLM: 1. Family
Therapy—methods. WM 430.5.F2 B864p]
RC488.5.B685 1987   616.89′156   87–18728
ISBN 0–205–11310–9

Printed in the United States of America

10 9 8 7 6 5 4 3 2 1   92 91 90 89 88 87

Dedicated to:
Jeanette, Jessica, Kelly, and Jordan
Marge, Jayne, Matt, and Clare

CONTENTS

≡ FOREWORD

Most writing in family therapy presents the reader with an established system of how to change families so as to relieve the symptoms they present or the stress they are suffering. The reader is encouraged to follow a rigid system and adopt one particular theoretical basis for bringing about change.

Brock and Barnard, two hands-on teachers, offer something different. They are sharing a kind of "clinical anthropologist's" view of what happens when a family interacts with an old-timer who has dallied with the fads but finds success in doing what works. There is precious little fluff in these pages. As each of the procedures is decribed, we capture anecdotal glimpses of family life and the process of family therapy. This is in keeping with the authors' intent, stated early on, that their work is not supposed to replace other texts and extensive study of family and therapy processes, but is designed to be used by those familiar with those terrains. The authors have gathered the data and organized it into a multifaceted notebook with value for both the young and more experienced therapist. The careful index lists many, many procedures so that the reader can use the book in a bed-table manner to ponder the procedures along with tomorrow's anxieties.

The casual style makes for easy reading. The usual trappings of high-bound solutions or invasive control of the process of change are avoided. The authors accurately sense and communicate that there is more than one potential solution to various situations but are willing to risk letting their ideas be made known to the professional community. The table of contents sets up a sort of encyclopedia of professional interaction patterns that is a gold mine for the developing therapist and a stimulant to the thinking of even the old hands in our territory.

Hidden behind the descriptions of what to do and when, one can see the message of gentle care offered to families in pain. Hidden also is a respectful awareness of each family as a unique culture that has evolved out of the blending of the parents' families of origin. Finally, I see throughout the book the integrity of the authors and their capacity to be peers with their students and with us, the readers.

Carl Whitaker, M.D.

═══ PREFACE

While teaching courses on marriage and family therapy and supervising casework, we became aware of the need for a resource that defined what we have come to know as procedures in professional family therapy practice. We asked our students to list what they needed to know, and then added our own items. Our intent from the outset was to create a reference for our students and for other professionals who see families in the context of their practices.

While this book will have particular value to therapists new to the field of family therapy, other professionals not trained in family therapy but who see families in the context of their practice will find it useful. We also believe the contents will be provocative and rewarding reading for the open-minded, seasoned clinician. We hope that our ideas will create new insights and new ways of perceiving commonly used approaches to clinical situations.

It is often said that theory provides a map with which to chart a route. As authors, supervisors, and therapists, each of us has a particular theoretical map that influenced the procedures described in this book. Our maps became clearer as we progressed through the writing. In a similar fashion, we believe the book provides an opportunity for the reader to discern the theoretical map he or she brings to therapy. We encourage you to closely examine those procedures you reject because it is likely that the reasons for rejection will yield more meaning than that for those embraced.

An objection sometimes raised about attempts to define procedure is that the role of the therapist is made trivial. We contend, however, that identifying what works enriches rather than diminishes any activity. By describing the generic ways of handling the most common situations faced by therapists, our goal is to help the field focus on that part of practice beyond the commonplace. Our interest is in freeing the clinician to creatively pursue new approaches. The body of procedure that develops in any field must constantly change, and we hope to aid that process by describing and cataloging standards that are meant to be challenged.

We are not so arrogant as to believe the procedures described here constitute the only way of accomplishing particular therapeutic objectives. We recognize that the field of family therapy has matured to the point of benefiting from many schools of thought, each with seemingly idiosyncratic ways of accomplishing therapeutic tasks. In spite of these supposed differences, we believe there are now some universally agreed ways of accomplishing many therapeutic tasks. We offer the procedures in this book as examples.

No book such as this one can include all the situations and predicaments that are encountered in therapy. Future editions will serve to mark another point in the process of identifying procedure. We certainly welcome the opportunity to hear and learn from readers' experience of the book and the application of the contents in therapy. We are particularly interested in learning about alternative procedures that are based on different theoretical foundations. Please use the addresses below to correspond with us directly.

In any undertaking of this kind, many people deserve thanks. From the time he learned of the project, John-Paul Lenney, our editor, was supportive of the idea that the field was ready for a book on procedure. It is rare to find an editor with training in family therapy. Consequently, his comments and ideas on the manuscript were especially helpful as was his kind way of letting us know what needed changing. Annette Joseph of Allyn and Bacon made sure things were done at the proper time and Maria Villanueva coordinated much needed copyediting services. The list is a long one of those who wrote the books and articles on which the field is based and who began the process of identifying procedure. We have profited from the good criticism of many reviewers including: Thomas E. Clark (Wake Forest University), Frederick G. Humphrey (University of Connecticut), Harvey Joanning (Texas Tech University), James F. Keller (Virginia Polytechnic Institute and State University), Lynne Kellner (L.U.K., Inc.) Luciano L'Abate (Georgia State University), Eleanor Macklin (Syracuse University), Fred P. Piercy (Purdue University), and Carl Whitaker. The support of our families was essential, and it is to them we dedicate this description of procedure in family therapy.

Gregory W. Brock, Ph.D.
Chairman, Department of Family Studies
University of Kentucky
Lexington, KY 40506–0054

Charles P. Barnard, Ed.D.
Director, Family Therapy Program
Clinical Services Center
University of Wisconsin-Stout
Menomonie, WI 54751

PROCEDURES
IN
FAMILY
THERAPY

≣ 1 ≣ OVERVIEW

INTRODUCTION

Clinical procedure in the field of family therapy traditionally has passed from master to apprentice through live observation and supervision. There are hints at procedure in family therapy literature, but nowhere has it been collected for easy access and use. Professions that have reached a high level of technical competence, however, have texts and manuals that specify the procedures to be used in specific practice situations. Lawyers, physicians, and ministers all have rich resources—their respective procedural manuals— much to the benefit of their daily practices. The profession and the discipline of family therapy have developed to such a degree that a procedural book for family therapists is an important and necessary addition to the literature.

Authors of family therapy texts have tended to emphasize the conceptual aspects of therapy rather than the procedural. Many texts, especially those with the word *technique* in the title, are so laden with theoretical notions that actual description of what is done to implement theory seems to have been forgotten. Where technique is specified, it is often stated in such a fuzzy manner that its use by the reader is likely to prove difficult at best and even dangerous when the author provides no real decision-making guidance. Many of the technique books are cookbooks that disguise the author's advocacy for a specific brand of family therapy. As a result, readers of the literature are exposed to many maps of theory without the means of traversing the obstacles encountered in therapy.

The purpose of this book is to specify and describe the important and effective procedures that experienced practitioners use in conducting family therapy. This is a how-to book, but it is not a cookbook. The terms *procedure* and *technique* are not synonymous. In this book, *procedure* connotes a refined and tested method that is meant to stand alone, outside of any specific

1

family therapy orientation. A group of procedures together might constitute a specific technique or therapeutic approach.

Family system theory is a valuable tool for assessing family problems and for designing overall treatment goals. The atheoretical, artful aspect of therapy, however, consists of what therapists do to carry out theory-based plans. They implement procedures that have developed out of their experience in attempting to use the various models of family therapy. These procedures are complex behavioral routines that tend to produce the same approximate result in terms of client behavior, and together the procedures define the practice of family therapy.

By recording at least some portion of what we teach our students and what we have found helpful to those who are attempting the difficult task of what we have found helpful, to those who are attempting the difficult task of supplying therapeutic services to families. The field of family therapy will benefit from a greater understanding of the procedural aspects of practice. Family therapists, as a result, will have a greater appreciation of the depth and breadth of skill demanded by effective and ethical practice. To date, the literature has neglected to perform this task.

ASSUMPTIONS AND UNDERLYING PHILOSOPHY

In writing this text, our assumptions about therapy and the role of the therapist became more apparent. Some are ordinary and some provocative, and naturally, not all procedures are in keeping with these assumptions; nonetheless, they are stated for your understanding.

1. The task of the family therapist is to change the structure and interaction processes of the client family.
2. The role of the therapist is that of the expert, and the therapist is responsible for the overall structure and process of therapy.
3. Clients are consumers of a service that is most effective when it is familiar to them and follows a format similar to that used by other professionals with whom clients have had prior contact.
4. As long as therapy remains within the bounds of ethical practice, there are no correct or incorrect procedures in family therapy; there are only outcomes which together produce change in family structure and processes.
5. The therapist's skill in using procedure is primarily the result of practice, self-study, and feedback based on observation by other practitioners.

HOW TO USE THIS BOOK

The book is not designed to be read from cover to cover. To best utilize it, first recognize the scope of the clinical situations and the procedures it covers. Of course, not all possible clinical situations and procedures are addressed. Nor will you find broad-based treatment strategies for problems such as eating disorders, drug abuse, etc. Knowing what situations *are* covered, however, will enable you to use this book as a generic resource, much as a writer uses a style manual.

After becoming familiar with the scope of the book, refer to it when you are faced with a new clinical situation or one that does not seem to be going well. Use the table of contents and the index to locate procedures of interest. If you cannot find your exact situation in the index, try to rephrase it in your mind as you continue to search. If your clinical situation is not addressed, look at a similar one, and you may discover a procedure that can be adapted.

We have attempted to write in a direct and descriptive manner. Early on, we decided that including citations and other means of identifying originators of the procedures would unnecessarily burden the text without any real gain in understanding. That does not mean we wish to claim the procedures as our intellectual property. Nor do we believe that the procedures are the property of anyone else. Procedure is the heritage of a profession and belongs to all its members. It is a labor in common.

≡ 2 ≡ INITIAL PHASE PROCEDURES

INTRODUCTION

The Western tradition of supplying mental health services is based on medical practice in which the first stage of treatment is diagnosis or assessment. Family therapy does not have a strongly developed diagnostic heritage compared to that of the field of psychology or psychiatry, although this area is developing. To design a treatment plan, each therapist must categorize, judge, and evaluate families.

Besides the actual process of therapy, one of the main distinguishing aspects of family therapy is its assessment procedure. The variables examined, the attitude of the therapist, and the cognitive map so often spoken about in family therapy texts all determine the style of treatment that has come to be known as family therapy. And it is during the treatment process that the accuracy of the assessment will be tested.

From the clinician's point of view, assessment is the process of getting to know enough about a family to make informed treatment decisions. More specifically, the procedure of assessment is the sequence of actions taken by the therapist designed to yield information about how the family operates and the function(s) of the presenting problems in the family organization. Whether assessment is therapeutic or not is a moot question in the psychotherapeutic context; it can be, depending on the skills and orientation of the clinician. The time spent in assessment, no matter how brief, should serve the dual purposes of diagnosis and therapy.

The steps in conducting an assessment are several. On first meeting with clients, social chitchat is common and necessary. Human relationships and social encounters tend to begin with small talk. It is nonthreatening and provides an opportunity to check out the other party. From the time the first meeting begins, the therapist collects information about how the family and its members function together. The small talk can be allowed to continue for as long a time as it produces important information.

While gathering this information, and throughout the assessment phase, the family therapist must *think*, not necessarily behave, in terms of family structure and family process. Delving too deeply into the intrapersonal functioning of one or more family members tends to misdirect the clinician's attention toward individuals and away from their social system. Forcing yourself to think in family-system terms is the key element in helping you to conduct family therapy rather than individual therapy in a group. This is not to say that the family therapist should not let individuals talk about their own problems, but that while they are talking and the therapist is attending, the therapist is also thinking about the family structure and the role individual problems play in the family system.

Some sort of executive remark is typically delivered by the therapist to make the transition from small talk to a focus on why the family is in therapy. "What brings you here?" might be one such remark. More typically, though, the therapist conducts the transition from chitchat to the task at hand by referring to the appointment phone call. This statement signals the family to begin talking about its problem(s), and that it what most families believe they are to do. Clinicians need to remember that clients who have not been in family therapy before tend to conduct themselves in accordance with stereotyped therapy sessions they have seen on TV or behave as they might in a physician's office. When families present themselves for therapy, they expect to be asked why they are there and to describe the problem(s) they are experiencing.

While the problem is being presented, the clinician attends to the processes revealed: Who begins first? Do family members talk for one another? Do they interrupt? Where are the alliances? Where is the seat of power? Who is the identified patient (IP)? The answers to all these questions and more are revealed during the problem presentation phase of the assessment. The clinician's questions serve the dual purpose of continuing the discussion and checking out hypotheses regarding the structure and function of the family and its symptoms. More experienced therapists tend to limit the amount of time devoted to describing the problem because experience allows them to arrive at hypotheses with less data. Less experienced therapists may need to devote more than one session to the assessment process.

DEVELOPING THE CLIENT RELATIONSHIP

≡ The Intake Telephone Call

Clinicians differ on the issue of involvement at the point of the initial phone call. Our preference is to be involved. Studies have demonstrated that the number of family members present at the initial session has definite implications regarding who will be present at future sessions. There is a far greater likelihood of ongoing commitments to therapy coming from those present in the first session than from those not present initially (who the clinician then attempts to lure in at a later time). For this reason, among others, the family therapist is well advised to take intake calls rather than having a secretary do so. This also places the therapist in a better position to initiate the battle for structure that Whitaker (Napier & Whitaker, 1978) calls essential. At the point of intake, the therapist can communicate who should attend the first session and begin to establish the tenor and structure of therapy.

For instance, assume the mother of three children calls about a concern regarding one child and states she wants a session alone to discuss this problem with the therapist. If the secretary takes the call and arranges for the requested individual session, the therapist runs the risk of the father and children perceiving the therapist and mother/wife as having an unfair alliance that will be difficult for them to surmount. Their mental set will pose another necessary struggle for the therapist that could have been avoided by having everyone present initially. The task of ensuring an ongoing commitment to the therapeutic alliance is enhanced if all are present from the outset.

The mother in the example may offer many reasons for coming alone, but the therapist should be steadfast in securing the presence of all without offending her. The following example illustrates a way of responding to the mother in this case:

> I realize the problem is primarily with your one child, and that your husband doesn't deal much with the children, but for me to be as helpful to you in this dilemma as I hope to be, I know from past experience it's best to have all present at least for this initial session. Hopefully you can understand and appreciate my desire to be as helpful as I can, and I know this is important. I know the schools will cooperate with allowing the children to be excused, and I would like to have you ask your husband to call me about whatever questions he might have in this regard. [Asking for the husband's phone number and then calling to explain your purpose is often valuable. It is amazing how often fathers cooperate when approached directly and communicated to with a respect that expresses their value and importance to the therapeutic effort.] I certainly could see you alone, and may choose to do that at a later point, but for this initial session I know it's important to have all present. We will need to trust one another, and while I know you don't know me yet, hopefully you can trust me on this count.

With this kind of presentation, it is exceptionally unusual to be met with ongoing apprehensiveness or a refusal to cooperate with the request. It seems that this type of request, while ensuring cooperation and attendance by all, also serves to engage the person on the other end of the phone conversation as they hear the desire to help communicated. It also seems to instill in clients an initial belief in the competence of the therapist. Naturally, these are important and valuable perceptions to have in place prior to the first session.

Once the family is present for the first session, ask the person who called to review what was discussed during the intake call. This serves to communicate that it is important for all to have the benefit of shared understanding, and, hopefully, it eliminates any concerns those not present during the call may have about that initial conversation. Continuing with the case example of the mother, the therapist might say something like: "Mrs. Jones, we spoke together about one week ago, and perhaps you can refresh my memory to make sure I understand what brings you in, and also we can make sure everyone understands the reason for your presence here today." After listening the therapist might choose to clarify points made in mother's presentation, or add things that seem to have been "forgotten." For instance, perhaps mother mentioned everything discussed, but forgot to mention that she wondered whether or not dad felt he might have anything to contribute to therapy. Perhaps she actually said that she wondered whether dad cared, but the therapist may choose to frame it as dad "wondering whether or not he had anything to contribute or if he could be helpful." At these times, reframing or packaging a message can be very helpful.

≡ Clarifying the Presenting Problem

Couples and families seen in clinical practice are frequently fragmented in many ways. They can present considerable disagreement over problem areas and differences in the intensity of their feelings about them. The clinician who does not make an extensive effort to clarify the presenting problem(s) is doomed to operating in as disoriented and fragmented a fashion as the dysfunctional family.

You have probably heard the old dictum: "A problem well defined is half solved." Although the literal meaning of this dictum may be an exaggeration, there is no doubt that clarifying the presenting problem is a significant clinical step. A reading of most of the original luminaries in the field of family therapy shows that fairly uniform agreement exists on the value of clarifying the presenting problem.

The clinician may find that there are as many presenting problems as there are individuals in the client group, and then some. For example, the individuals in the group may have their own respective ideas about what the problem is and what needs change. The clinician may also observe various problems not mentioned before by the family members; for example, the fact that there is no shared agreement; there is little, if any, effective listening;

some strong silencing mechanisms are quite evident; or one or more family members evidence significant affect which is not even presented as a problem.

The act of delineating the problems of a dysfunctional and chaotic family can often be the first therapeutic intervention. Simply clarifying the family members' issues can prove helpful as they begin to understand what has been contributing to the chaos they experience. Frequently it is helpful to label the various identified problems as clutter that prevents the clients from securing the kind of family/marital life they hope for. Once the clutter is identified, you can determine where to initially direct efforts to eliminate it from the family operation. It is important to be sensitive to addressing problems that are reasonably defined and lend themselves to easy resolution. Further, initially intervening with the problems most likely to be resolved will provide family members with the sense of success and mastery that likely has been absent from their lives.

"I want him to love me more." This type of problem statement is more likely to be resolved when the problem is defined in more specific behavioral terms such as: "I would like him to talk with me for five minutes after dinner, or sometime before we go to bed, rather than just watch TV." "I would like him to help me put the two youngest children to bed three nights a week." Initially breaking problems down into manageable pieces makes it far more likely that everyone will realize what is necessary for success. In selecting those pieces of a problem that are most likely to ensure a sense of accomplishment, it is often wise to negotiate which one seems most reasonable to focus on initially. This process of clients negotiating which piece to address first can provide further evaluation data to the clinician, and it also frequently provides an opportunity to do some effective therapeutic management of communication/negotiation processes and skills.

The process of clarifying the problem also provides the couple/family with a sense of the clinician's competence and capacity for appropriately managing their otherwise destructive process. Although the client's perception that care emanates from the therapist has been extensively acknowledged to be important, the "test of competence" seems just as important, if not more so, in work with families. In fact, if this sense of competence is not perceived by clients, why should they extend the effort and money necessary to keep future appointments?

Each person present should be afforded the opportunity to express what the problem is or what needs to be changed. Framing or defining the problem as "what needs to be changed" conveys the valuable metamessage that the focus of therapy is change. Each succeeding session can then be initiated with a statement such as: "What have you changed since we were last together?" This statement also underscores the notion that the family is responsible for the process of change and keeps the initiative for change with them.

Another point to consider regarding clarification of the problem is "Why now?" In most cases the problems presented are not acute in nature, but have been present for some considerable period of time. To determine what brings the family members in at *this* time can provide valuable information for the clinician about their attempts to resolve the problem(s) on their own. A good sense of just how creative the group members are will become evident. Also, the clinician will learn what approach not to attempt with them, because the family implemented a solution and it failed.

A last point for consideration involves determining and changing the family's perceptual context of the problem. To assess this area, think along the lines of a "bad-sad" continuum. If a family member identifies another member's problem in terms that might be called "bad"—angry, mean, bitchy, vindictive—framing the problem as possibly being stimulated by "sad" factors—hurt, depressed, lonely, isolated—can be beneficial. This shift in perception of the problem's basis often proves extremely valuable in introducing greater flexibility and increasing the likelihood of problem resolution as therapy progresses. Certainly great sensitivity must be exercised in this area so that a person with a heavy investment in perceiving a problem in a particular way does not end up feeling abused by the therapist.

≡ Conducting a Genogram

The genogram as an assessment tool has been around for a long time. Its symbols and mapping technique were popularized by Murray Bowen, and the genogram procedure is endorsed and described in nearly every family therapy text. Consequently, many clinicians use the genogram in the initial stage of therapy to assess family history and as a way to get acquainted.

The structure of a genogram is relatively straightforward. The therapist can best begin the process by spending several minutes explaining (1) the rationale for the genogram (a means of getting acquainted that involves gathering information about families of origin in order to better understand how family background influences current family issues), (2) what clients will be asked to do (answer questions and share insights about one another's families), (3) how long the genogram will last (thirty to forty-five minutes), and (4) the sequence of events (who goes first).

Typically, unless the therapist selects someone to begin, the person who made the appointment will do so. From a relationship-building point of view, however, it is often better if the spouse less interested in therapy is asked to go first. Hopefully, through increased client-therapist interaction during the relatively nonthreatening task of the genogram, the less interested spouse will become more interested in and committed to therapy. The spouse more willing to begin can be chosen if the therapist believes that requesting the less interested spouse to begin will harm the therapeutic relationship at this initial stage. In either case, the less interested spouse cannot be allowed to merely sit by while his or her partner works with the therapist. All family members, especially children, are to be fully involved at all times and enlisted as consultants to the therapist.

The genogram process usually consists of mapping out one family of origin at a time. A large drawing area such as a blackboard or newsprint tablet is very helpful. Clients and therapists alike retain more interest in the experience and find it more meaningful when they can actually see the structure of the families they are talking about. In addition, diagramming the family structures is the primary method of keeping an entire family involved. It provides a focal point for those members not talking at a given time and allows them to think about someone else's family.

In some styles of therapy, a great amount of detail is gathered during the genogram. Dates of marriages, deaths, divorces, births, and ages of family members across as many generations as possible are dutifully written down. For the genogram commonly used in the initial phase of therapy, however, less is more might be the guiding dictum. A more efficient procedure is to concentrate on the current and immediately previous generations, asking everyone to help map out all the current and past members of the system and obtaining their current ages and the approximate dates of important events such as deaths, marriages, and divorces. This need not take more than a few minutes, and it should not be the client's primary focus. The most useful information produced by the genogram is not the family structure but the nature of the relationships making up the structure.

The therapist must direct the spouses to consider the influences from their families of origin that affect the style of their marriage. For example, to gain understanding of the model of marriage displayed to a couple by their parents, ask each person questions such as, "How did your parents show affection?" "What was their social life like?" and "What did they do when they disagreed with each other?" To assess the parental model ask: "With which parent did you spend the most time?" "What was the emotional climate of the relationship?" "How did you show irritation toward one another?" and "How was affection displayed?" Questions about the closest parent are especially important, because it is reasonable to assume that the style of relationship developed with the closest parent or caretaker will be the style of relationship sought with a marital partner. Other areas to assess could include role rigidity, power allocation, communication of warmth and empathy, alliances, techniques of adaptation, and major illnesses.

There are several points to keep in mind while conducting a genogram. Because it is often an initial task of therapy, the clinician needs to maintain the involvement of all the family members throughout the experience. Typically, one branch of the family tree is dealt with at a time, and it is easy to spend too much time following the unnecessary strategy of asking questions of one spouse or family member to the exclusion of the others present. After a minute or so spent talking with one person, you can ask another person to agree, disagree, or share a comment about the other's family. Questions such as "Is that your perception?" or "How do you see her (his) family?" can serve this purpose. All members of a family need to be kept involved and can be, as everyone is asked to participate.

Second, because the genogram is usually an introduction to therapy, the experience can be light and even humorous, depending on the wit of the therapist. The material generated by clients needs to be taken seriously, of course, but a little humor can help avoid a dull, question-and-answer grilling that frustrates therapists and clients alike. Third, and most important, the genogram presents an excellent opportunity for the therapist to demonstrate professional competence. At least one study (Brock & Sanderson, 1984) has suggested that clients determine the competence of their therapist in the first session in part by how much they learn about themselves, their family, and family dynamics in general. The genogram presents an ideal opportunity for the therapist to make statements with this point in mind.

For example, if both spouses are firstborn children, a therapist could remark, "We tend to find that firstborn children are more ambitious than later siblings and as a result, I would guess that you two are not only ambitious but also fairly competitive with one another." Or, if one spouse's family of orientation is large and the other spouse is an only child, the therapist could remark, "I imagine you, John, were attracted to the stimulation and activity of her larger family while you, Mary, were attracted to the simplicity and quiet of his family." These remarks or interpretations need not be earthshaking, brilliant insights into the psyche of either spouse.

It is important for therapists to share their thoughts and conclusions about the families described by their clients. Clients are hungry to learn, and such comments not only allow therapists to investigate perceptions, but also often produce insight about the family, benefiting both the therapist and the family members. During a genogram that is illuminating to clients, a therapist will often hear one client state to another, "So, that's why you are like that" or "I never knew that." Comments such as these bring clients back for the second session.

Teaching clients about themselves, their family, and about families in general has the equally important goal of maintaining a balance of social exchange during the initial phase of therapy. The therapy relationship, like other interpersonal relationships, proceeds through several phases, the first of which is a getting-acquainted period. In this phase, the participants (therapist and client) exchange information about themselves verbally and nonverbally. The exchanges occur on a rapid and short-term basis, and the balance of debits and credits in the relationship is kept carefully balanced. Deferred gratification or exchange imbalance in the early stage of a relationship often produces emotional withdrawal by one participant. For example, the person sitting next to you on a long bus ride over-discloses and you feel more and more emotionally distant as the imbalance in self-disclosure increases.

Such a social exchange imbalance does not usually play a healthy role in relationships until the participants have established a foundation of trust produced by short-term, balanced exchange. Therefore, in the initial phase of therapy, the therapist needs to attend to the balance of exchange, and one good way to maintain the balance is to share observations and insights that come to mind during the genogram with the family. Many therapists merely ask clients questions without giving back information that will help to maintain the balance of social exchange during the initial interview. The full potential of the genogram is not achieved by limiting its purpose to merely collecting information.

≡ Collecting Relationship History

A number of authors have written excellent descriptions of the ways to conduct the relationship history portion of the initial phase of therapy. Stahmann and Heibert (1977) have presented the Structured Initial Interview for married couples in which the areas to ask about are detailed. Weber, McKeever, and McDaniel (1985) have defined a model for family interviews. The comments below are meant as additions to history taking/assessment models presented in the literature.

Initial Attraction
Couples who are in the midst of turmoil focus intensely on what is wrong with their relationship and each other. By initiating a discussion of how they met and what attracted them, a break in such negative attention is forced. Most often, they will cooperate fully, and the resulting discussion is a pleasant one. Since they have been asked similar questions many times in the past, however, the therapist must help the partners get past their ritualized answers to questions such as, "How did you meet?" When they are permitted to answer only with their ritualized answers, little is accomplished.

The initial phase of therapy, which usually involves asking such questions, is the best time to make it understood that therapy will consist of more than the same old disclosures. Asking for detail is one way to get past the ritualized answers. For example, the therapist might say something like, "Surely, there was more to it than that." Through this type of encouragement, partners can receive the specific guidance needed to disclose their feelings and thoughts about each other that they have not shared previously.

Expectations of a Marital Partner
Some therapists place geat emphasis on discovering the expectations each partner had about a marital partner prior to marriage. Unfortunately, these expectations probably were not at all well articulated at that time. Consequently, clients usually have difficulty responding to the question,

"What expectations did you have of a wife (husband) when you married?" It is often easier to identify such expectations using the material generated by a genogram than to ask clients to state them. If a genogram is not conducted as part of the assessment process, clients can be asked to compare their parents' marital roles with how they expected their spouse to behave. Such comparisons help the discussion of expectations to be less abstract. Some clients will honestly state that they had no expectations, and they will need help to understand that although they may not have sat down and drawn up a list, they did want a spouse to behave in a certain manner.

Courtship History

The courtship phase of the relationship is best discussed by referring to major events such as first intercourse, first item purchased together, major fights and the like, that both spouses probably remember. The events discussed should be restricted to those both remember. Otherwise, the topic may shift to, "Why don't you remember that?" and create hurt feelings, and at this phase of therapy, the emphasis should be on helping a couple remember the positive reasons they chose to marry.

Significant Events During Marriage

In the same manner, the history of the marriage can be discussed. It is helpful to use a blackboard to create a time line of events to give couples perspective on how much they have been through together. These discussions can become labored and lengthy unless the therapist helps prevent the spouses from telling story after story. Usually, one spouse tells a story while the other listens. The key to maintaining control of the session is to stay actively involved by asking questions of both spouses regarding the event. Their stories will become abbreviated and the nonparticipating spouse will not be able to disengage from the session. Also, when the therapist has heard enough about an event, the couple or family should be encouraged to move on and not allowed to ramble; for example, saying "Let's go on to the next event" or asking "What was the next major event?" is appropriate.

≡ Explaining the Purpose of Therapy

Most clients enter family therapy without a clear idea of what will happen or what they are to do. They are usually anxious and unsure how to act. As a result, many clients may seem defensive or actively resist the therapy. The intitial session is a good time to put client fears to rest by describing the process and goals of family therapy.

The description should not be long or complicated. It should also be stated in language that children as well as adults can understand. The following is an example:

I'd like to take a few minutes to talk about family therapy so that we all understand what we are doing and where we are going. Families are very important to each of you, and to me, and to all of us. All families have rules that tell us what is OK and not OK. They also have roles to help get things done so that everyone in the family understands who they are and what they are to do. When a family is not working well or one family member has problems, we have found that the rules and roles need to be changed so the family helps everyone grow as a person.

Family therapy usually has two parts. First, I need to get to know your family, its history, its rules, its roles, and how you do things together. Then we will all talk about what needs changing. In the second part of therapy, we will work together to make changes. I want to emphasize that in family therapy we don't blame any one person for the problems you are having. Also, we will need everyone's help in making changes.

The objective of describing family therapy to clients is to provide them with an overview so therapy has structure and meaning.

≡ Presenting the Concept of Family System

Through all phases of therapy, many new concepts may be presented to clients. In the initial phase of therapy, the concept of family system is often defined to help clients differentiate between family therapy and individual therapy. In the middle phase, the same concept can be used as the rationale for a reframing of presenting symptoms and other family problems. In the terminal phase of therapy, the concept is helpful in clarifying what changes in family organization may be necessary to accommodate upcoming developmental crises in family life. Teaching families about the concept of family system is a prudent investment of session time, if a therapist is able to define the concept clearly.

A number of methods have been described in the literature to aid in defining the family system concept. Analogies are helpful, and the most popular is the mobile. Many family therapists have made or purchased a mobile comprised of family figures so that when one figure is moved, all others move. When the family system is defined, the therapist can easily demonstrate not only that all family members affect one another, but also that change in one member does not necessarily mean an equal change in others. Family members may change more or less, depending on how directly they are connected to the figure that is moved. The mobile is also helpful should the concept of homeostasis needs to be defined.

The principal task of defining any concept is to use language that the clients readily understand. Family therapy buzzwords such as circular causality, linear casuality, morphogenesis, role, dyad, parental marriage, etc., are not appropriate, even if the client family is made up of family therapists. An appropriate definition of the family system concept might proceed like this:

I think it is important here in the beginning of therapy to let you know how I think about families.

Families are like that mobile hanging above my desk. Every figure is connected to others. Notice that all the other figures move if I move this figure. Some move more than others , but they all move.

Your family is like the mobile, because everyone is connected, and when someone in the family changes, everyone else adjusts or also changes to some degree. For example, if one of you should win the Reader's Digest Sweepstakes, everyone in the family would feel the impact of all that money. Likewise, with the problems you are experiencing, everyone has had to change, some of you perhaps for the better, and others for the worse.

To work on the issues bringing you into therapy, no one will be blamed for causing the problems, because all of you have been changed by these issues, and changing is now everyone's responsibility and privilege. That is why the whole family is here in therapy. Everyone will need to help out if we are to get anywhere. Does everyone understand?

This statement serves a number of purposes. First, a new way of thinking about family life is introduced. Second, every member of the family is given responsibility for change, without having to feel responsible for the problems. Lastly, the need to have the entire family present in therapy is explained. The question at the end of the statement provides an opportunity for family members to comment on the thoughts presented and to reveal whether they will cooperate in the therapy.

The therapist may speak of triangles, alliances, coalitions, boundaries, and many other terms that label and describe family organization. As a result of using these new labels and concepts, the reframing and relabeling of symptoms and presenting problems become possible. Reframing and relabeling can be conducted without using family organization concepts, but both are much easier if clients are educated in foundation concepts such as the family system.

≡ Establishing a Relationship with Clients

Establishing a relationship, also termed *joining*, is a complicated process that begins the moment either the therapist or the client becomes psychologically aware of the other. From this always sketchy beginning, the therapeutic relationship develops as an adjunct or impediment to family change.

It is important to realize that clients who are undertaking therapy for the first time, as well as those with past therapy experience, expect to have the same form of relationship they have developed with other professionals. Unfortunately, most of us have learned to be wary of dentists; we also lie to our physicians and ignore their advice. Unless clients learn that a new sort of relationship is required for family therapy, it may not be successful.

The nature of all therapy demands that the relationship be warm, empathic, and genuine. Carl Rogers (1951) defined these conditions as necessary and sufficient for individual therapy, and training in how to create such relationship conditions has been part of graduate programs for many years. As defined by Minuchin and Fishman (1981) and many others, work with families and married couples requires more, especially in the initial phase of therapy.

Since the client is usually a group of individuals and the problems discussed usually focus on the actions of family members, the awful truth of relationships emerges quickly compared with the pace of disclosure in individual therapy. The relationship needed to support disclosure of family problems is perceived as safe, not confrontative initially, and yet, because clients come to therapy expecting guidance and advice in addition to a sympathetic ear, the therapist needs to be seen as an expert in therapy and not just family life.

Family therapy tends to be action oriented; that is, the therapist introduces new ideas as well as new behavior in the session. Therapists need to redefine and relabel symptoms; thus, persuasion and selling ideas is important. To be persuaded or to accept alternate conceptions of family patterns and symptoms, clients must be confident that going along with their therapist will pay off. Family therapists are familiar with how to act warm and empathic, but very little has been written for us about how to inspire client confidence.

As in any relationship, therapist self-confidence is the best determinant of client confidence in the therapist and is displayed in a number of ways, including diplomas hung on the office wall and the office furnishings. Behaviorally, therapists display confidence through movement, dress, and voice quality. In addition, clients become more confident in their therapist as a result of the authoritative statements made in therapy sessions.

Authoritative statements are those that educate clients about their family and themselves. For example, while listening to a family member describe their reactions to a recent death in the family, the therapist might comment, "What you are referring to is a grief reaction to sudden loss. We often go through a series of stages, beginning with denial and then anger, after a sudden loss." In this instance, the therapist is sharing knowledge and expertise with the client. While such statements should not make up the majority of what a therapist says in therapy, statements that are intended to educate the client demonstrate therapist competence and create confidence.

≡ Establishing Therapeutic Goals

Establishing goals is every bit as important for the therapist as it is for the family. For the therapist, goal establishment helps achieve feedback about the impact of interventions. Such feedback can be significant in preventing the burnout that stems from a sense of aimlessness. Without some specific direction and focus, it is easy for a therapist to question effectiveness, especially if a family or couple questions the value of therapy. Typically, this type of questioning and doubt is unproductive, harming the therapist's sense of well-being and purpose, not to mention the family's confidence. A lack of specificity helps the family keep the therapist off balance so that no change is effected, and an undertone of anger and resentment that benefits no one is engendered.

Establishing goals also serves to better ensure a clear understanding by all involved of such parameters as what might be necessary to effect desired change and how long it might take. This focus proves very therapeutic to many families who are fragmented and feeling diffuse regarding their own understanding. Naturally, a sense of diffusion can be a part of the problem itself.

In the first session, it is important to establish the tone of purposefulness by having the family identify what they hope to change/accomplish in therapy. It is important at this time to encourage as much specificity as possible, recognizing that it will probably be difficult because of the masking related to present and past emotions that occurs. For instance, when a wife claims through her tears that she wants her husband to "love me more," it is important to help her define her needs operationally. An effective way of doing this is to ask her, "What would you see or hear from him that is different from how things currently are, that would result in your believing he does love you more?" Vague responses such as, "If only he wouldn't look at me with that look he gets on his face" need greater specificity: "Would you describe his look to me now?" "When does that look appear?" "All right, now what else would be different that would help you believe in his love for you?" Pursuing this type of information might provoke anxiety and/or anger in the client, and it is often helpful to diminish this potential by inserting a statement such as, "I realize my questions may seem irrelevant to you, and may even result in your feeling frustrated, but I need you to bear with me as I try to be helpful." The effect of this statement can often be enhanced by inserting a recognition of the feelings the client is presenting, saying, for instance, "I know you are hurting and probably feeling some resentment and frustration, but I need to do this to be helpful to you," and then continuing.

Some families or couples may be vague and have trouble identifying specific goals. In such a case, the therapist might suggest that all meet together for another one to three sessions to complete an assessment and to determine goals and the best way to proceed. Having several sessions allows clients time to better organize themselves as they respond to the new structure provided by the therapist and therapy. Also, the therapist is provided with an opportunity to proceed without having to accept the nebulous contract that might evolve by simply accepting the clients' ambiguity. Such a compromise by a therapist could hamper future effectiveness.

The purpose of this agreed-upon assessment phase is to identify goals of ongoing therapy to be negotiated. Client vagueness needs to be accepted at first to avoid amplifying their uneasiness and frustration prematurely. The therapist might explain, "The importance of these struggles and concerns to you is evidenced by your reluctance to identify specific concerns too quickly. That is encouraging, and for that reason I am willing to take a few sessions to attempt to determine what might be most helpful to you." The assessment phase can then continue, as the effort is completed to have clients specify what they want changed. This process also serves to metacommunicate to the couple/family that the therapist perceives that therapy exists to effect change and that the goal of change is paramount. New goals may surface as therapy proceeds, so negotiating time parameters as part of the therapeutic contract is valuable (see following section, "Establishing a Therapeutic Contract").

≡ Establishing a Therapeutic Contract

Family therapists who espouse a brief, problem-specific orientation will inevitably want to develop a contract that specifies therapy goals. Although these therapists promote clear, explicit goal statements, others act in a less defined fashion. Thus far, no research has suggested that one style is superior to the other; thus, each therapist is left to decide the form of the therapeutic contract, and what importance to attach to it.

For the beginning family therapist, developing more specific and problem-focused therapeutic contacts seems to be valuable. Such contracts provide them with an opportunity to more clearly assess the movement that is occurring with the family and the effectiveness of various interventions employed. The family also benefits, because it has identified criteria to use in determining change. Often, family members seem to work at cross-purposes, using different criteria to assign value to what occurs in therapy. The establishment of a shared set of criteria to assess achievement of goals can be therapeutic by itself for some of these families. Also, in the process of negotiating an initial contract with the family, the therapist is provided with a rich opportunity to observe how the family is organized and how it operates. Many questions may be answered during the negotiation of a contract such as: Who speaks to whom and about what? What affect seems evident as various concerns are discussed? How do various members exercise influence in the family?

Issues such as the frequency and length of meetings and the family's expectations about therapy and the therapist should be determined during contract negotiation. The negotiation of these issues can quickly address the battle for initiative, or the question of who is to do what work to induce change in the family. The family members may believe that all they need to do is make their scheduled appearances and the therapist/therapy will somehow magically resolve their issues. They may be entering therapy tentatively, because the last two therapists they were engaged with were inappropriately confrontational. One contract used often is to meet one to three times to assess and develop an understanding, realizing that at the end of this agreed-upon time, all members decide whether therapy should proceed. Naturally, the therapist has a vote in proceeding or not, just as the family members do. At the end of a few initial sessions an agreement is arrived at regarding whether to proceed or not, and if so, for what purposes or goals, how long sessions should continue to address these goals before another evaluation, and, what everyone's expectations are in this process.

This type of minimal contract provides all with some clarity of purpose and promotes commitment to the therapy. Working in a contractual framework, or within chunks of time, also provides everyone with a sense of increased freedom to end by choice, rather than a feeling that termination is arrived at in some cumbersome fashion or by simply not appearing for appointments. This sense of freedom to terminate can be particularly valuable for those families or family members who are uneasy and tentative about committing themselves to therapy. For such clients, addressing the element of time seems particularly important, because then their preconceived notions of therapy's being endless (or lasting for years, at best) can be dispelled. Also, by specifying issues to be addressed, the therapist can resolve the clients' notion that therapy is magical or something done to them. While negotiating a contract, the family therapist can describe what might be expected of clients in the way of homework, any paper-and-pencil assessment tasks that may be employed, types of in-session tasks the family may be asked to engage in, whether all members will be present at all sessions or if various subsystems will be seen in isolation, the role of consultants or aids such as videotaping and one-way mirrors, and so on. This type of information often promotes a sense of comfort for the family members, so that they more quickly invest in therapy.

ASSESSMENT CONCEPTS AND PROCEDURES

☰ Family Readiness for Therapy

Recognizing that families are composed of individuals, it is important to acknowledge that family readiness for change, in varying degrees, lies within each member. Consequently, the clinician needs to assess the level of readiness or motivation of each member in order to avoid making therapeutic moves that would alienate those least motivated. Along with each member's level of readiness, the clinician needs to be alert to the individual's power or potency within the family organization.

The clinician who is unaware of individuals' levels of readiness and power could easily end up not only being unsuccessful in drawing families into therapy, but may actually push them out. For example, the clinician who does not adequately assess that the father is minimally invested in therapy, but is very powerful in the family's organization, may prematurely take the mother's side on an issue and provoke the father into sabotaging any return to "that damn therapist." While the clinician's professional ego may be temporarily bruised, the real loser is the family that sought help in the tenuous and uncertain way that most families enter therapy.

The clinician needs to direct more intensive engagement procedures toward family members who seem least ready for therapy and toward those who are most powerful and influential in the family. Continuing the above example, it would be important to direct engagement efforts toward the father, who appears to be the least ready or committed to the treatment effort, but is a powerful decision-maker with regard to influencing the family's behavior. To quickly take sides with the mother may be too dramatic a change for the father to adapt to, and may also be an affront to his belief about how his role should be regarded: Father is most important. For these reasons, the clinician would probably best engage father by initially being responsive to his perception of the family structure and rules. By doing so, the clinician can also begin to create shock absorbers in the relationship with the father that will facilitate confrontations with him that may later become important. Without the development of these shock absorbers, dad may never evidence any more than the minimal readiness already displayed, and the clinician, then, will never experience the benefit of having firmer therapeutic leverage than that present initially.

Readiness can be assessed by asking questions such as, "How did you decide to come here?" "What do you hope will change by being here?" "Recognizing how uncomfortable it can be to come to therapy, what motivates you to be here?" Often it can prove very valuable to ask several family members to answer these questions as though they were someone else in the family. For instance, the clinician may ask the youngest daughter, "Do you think mom really wants to be here?" Assuming the daughter responds affirmatively, a natural follow-up would be, "And what do you think mom hopes can be changed by coming here?" This type of questioning can provide much insight to the family members present, as well as to the clinician. Frequently, such a discussion is the first opportunity family members have had to learn how they are perceived by each other and what beliefs are harbored by each member.

Along with responses to questions such as these, the clinician can assess readiness by observing behaviors such as an apparent eagerness to talk, an authentic and pleasant self-presentation, the presence of tears that seem to communicate a sense of hopefulness or desperation, a warm greeting at the outset or a sincere "thank you" at the end of a session, and comments that convey an individual's readiness to accept personal responsibility for family difficulties rather than to project all blame to others. Although clinicians are frequently heard making statements such as, "I can just sense they are ready," it is likely that specific observed behaviors, such as those just identified, are the source of the clinician's sense of family readiness for therapy.

≡ Family Structure and Function Indicators

One of the goals of the assessment process is to determine the health of the family system. The process demands that the therapist make value judgements in which the client family, its structure, and interaction processes are compared to a model family or against some standard familiar to the therapist. Like it or not, all therapists use such a standard, and all therapists make value judgements about the functioning of their clients. The primary issue here is the makeup of the standard used to define the optimally functioning family. We suggest one that fits with the cultural milieu of the place where the family resides or one that the family identifies with.

The healthy, optimally functioning family has been ignored, to a large extent, in the family therapy literature, but it has received attention from family scientists such as Walsh (1982). If the research on healthy families is distilled into primary functions and indicators of those functions (an onerous task conducted by Lee Walker, 1978), we arrive at six general areas of functioning and a set of descriptive guidelines. These can be used to compare the health of a client family with that of the optimally functioning family by observing and rating client families in each of the six areas. This helps to maintain the focus of therapy on family functioning and to segment family processes into parts easier to observe and evaluate. The six areas of functioning are: (1) roles, (2) emotional expression, (3) interdependence/individuation, (4) power, (5) communication, and (6) subsystems.

Roles are repetitive patterns of individual behavior and serve functional purposes in day-to-day family life. Roles delineate the family's structure and maintain the family's interactional processes.

Optimal Family Roles
1. Clear differentiation exists between the roles of parent, child, and spouse.
2. Roles may be shared, reversed, or changed, depending on the situation.
3. New roles can be tried out or old ones modified.
4. The roles taken by family members complement one another.
5. These roles are also similar across situations and members.
6. Parents share child care.

Emotional expression refers to the notion that each family has an emotional tone that is based on the degree of emotional expressiveness, sensitivity, and responsiveness family members share with each other. Families also create norms of reciprocity that govern reflexive patterns of emotional expression.

Optimal Family Emotional Expression
1. The overall emotional tone of the family is positive.
2. Family members are sensitive to one another's feelings.
3. The rules for expressing emotion are clear, and the expression of emotion tends to be spontaneous.
4. Expression of negative emotions is allowed as well as sensitivity toward others.
5. The amount of expressiveness is high, with laughter, humor, and warmth evident.
6. Open and unresolved hostility is absent.
7. The family tolerates and encourages the expression of a wide range of feelings.

Interdependence/individuation refers to the amount of autonomy or individuation granted to the individual by the family.

Optimal Family Individuation
1. Each individual has separate recreational and social activities.
2. Family members discuss individual problems and understand and support one another.
3. Different value systems are tolerated in the family; however, central values concerning sexuality, money, religion, work ethics, and family loyalty are jointly held.
4. Cooperation rather than competition is a family value.

5. Interpersonal relationships with nonfamily members are approved of as long as family routine is not disturbed.
6. The family members take responsibility for their individual behavior and feelings.
7. Differences of opinion are tolerated, and mutual agreement is frequently the product of discussions.

Power can be defined as the degree of influence or control family members have over each other. The use of power and its distribution among family members is very important to the understanding and changing of dysfunctional interaction patterns.

Optimal Family Power Distribution
1. Everyone has input into family decisions.
2. Family members seek and take leadership in different aspects of family life, and other family members willingly follow such leadership.
3. Power in the family is centralized within the parental dyad.
4. Family rules are enforced through persuasion rather than through intimidation or force. Violence is not tolerated.
5. There is little hostile, angry, acting-out behavior. Conflicts tend to be open, and they are resolved quickly.
6. Except for the parental dyad, coalitions among family members are open and short-term.

Communication is concerned with the delivery and reception of verbal and nonverbal information between family members. It includes skills in exchanging patterns of information within the family system.

Optimal Family Communication
1. A high volume of information seeking and sharing occurs between family members.
2. Nonverbal and verbal messages are congruent, and the intent of messages is clear and open.
3. Silence is infrequent, and the family deals with a wide range of topics.
4. Conflicts are resolved through discussion.
5. Most family communication is positive in tone.
6. All family members are capable of using problem-solving statements that encourage the efficient resolution of conflicts.

Also important are the subsystems (or subgroupings) within the family and how they maintain the family system. The types of subsystems include the parent, spouse, and sibling groups, and the alliances between and among the members of the groups.

Optimal Family Subsystems

1. The boundaries between the parental, spousal, and sibling subsystems are clear.
2. Each subsystem performs its functions adequately.
3. There are strong emotional bonds between subsystems and between the individuals within subsystems.
4. The parental subsystem leads the family and holds most of the power.
5. Individuals within subsystems participate in shared activities.
6. Coalitions across subsystems occur but are short-term.

Naturally, families with sources of identity and cultural heritage differing from that of middle- and upper-income North Americans must be evaluated with guidelines somewhat different from those stated here. However, one basic assumption of family therapy is that all families work approximately the same way. The therapist should not stray wildly from the general guidelines for optimal family functioning.

≡ Indicators of Resistance

Resistance is the act of being in opposition to or avoiding something. More recent analytically oriented writers such as Anderson and Stewart (1983) regard resistance differently than writers such as Erickson (see Haley, 1973), Watzlawick, Weakland, and Fisch (1974), and de Shazer (1982). The latter authors' views on resistance most adequately represent our own view, which is that the construct of resistance is much ado about nothing.

We must remember that what we call resistance is a two-person phenomenon; a relationship between persons must exist before any behaviors can be identified as resistance. We must keep in mind the utilitarian value of this construct: As long as this concept is available, we can avoid responsibility and project the blame for lack of progress onto our clients by saying, "They are just too resistant!"

Resistance as a two-person phenomenon means that we have some responsibility for its existence or nonexistence. To avoid resistance, the therapist must maintain a sense of balance within the client relationship and, in addition, the potential for retreating and regrouping with the client group. This is particularly important in the early stages of therapy when the relationship with the client has not developed sufficiently to serve as a shock absorber for direct confrontation. Once this shock-absorbing quality is present in the form of a relationship commitment, behaviors reflecting resistance are far less likely.

Retreating and regrouping with the client group refers to the capacity to sense client irritation likely to be counterproductive, and then to make necessary shifts such that a more productive interaction can occur. Rather than engaging in battle, employ the philosophy and technique of judo: The opponent's force is not opposed by an action of equal force but is accepted and then amplified by first yielding to it and then going with it. For example, assume that during the initial session someone appears to be very antagonistic and irritated. Perhaps the clinician has provoked it or maybe something totally unrelated to the therapy has. Whatever the case, the wise therapist will initiate moves that will effectively neutralize this potentially problematic behavior. One way is to identify with the client by agreeing with a statement said or a point made, perhaps even by placing yourself in a symmetrical relationship with the client, saying: "I can see that you and I are going to get along well because we are so much alike. I often feel and think just as you do, and I don't have the opportunity to meet many like us." The goal is to change the interaction that is apparently becoming oppositional or resistive to interaction that is more cooperative and potentially productive.

Not infrequently, entire client groups that do not follow through with assigned tasks or activities are identified as being resistant. Again, it is much easier for us as professionals to define them as resistant than it is to realize that we have blundered in not providing them with sufficient understanding, skills, or motivation to be cooperative and successful. Or, the family that seemingly refuses to talk as freely as the clinician might like is referred to as resistant, without the clinician even considering that this family is not accustomed to talking with strangers about their problems. Perhaps the family has been cautioned about going too quickly with therapists "because they tell everything to the courts" by neighbors whose therapist had to report them to the local social service unit for physically abusing a child. What is more important is to observe the clients' behaviors, then define them as cooperative and reaffirm them. For instance, with family members that refuse to talk, we might thank them for being courteous and demonstrate our appreciation for having clients who "think before they talk, because so many don't." Further, they can be acknowledged for caring about themselves and their family so much that they exercise "good, cautious judgement." These efforts at retreating and regrouping will effectively eliminate the occurrence of behaviors conveniently referred to as resistance.

Whenever therapists find themselves wanting to refer to a family or couple as resistant, they should stop and ask: "What could I be doing differently with these people to foster cooperation and further enhance our relationship?" As the relationship improves, behaviors typically characterized as resistance will not likely occur.

≡ Family Rules

Rules are part of every relationship, and family rules are the dynamic components of the family's organization. The obvious rules govern who takes out the garbage, who mows the lawn, who does which housecleaning task, and the like, but numerous rules of a more subtle nature exist. They are the internalized implicit regulations that maintain a family's systemic functioning, valuable to know in developing a therapeutic plan.

Ideally, this plan, though responsive to the family's present rules, will facilitate the development of more functional ones. Ignoring the family's rules could provoke premature termination. For example, the family that functions with the rule of not acknowledging or responding to mother's intense, depressive behaviors may abruptly terminate if the undiscerning clinician comments on it without first having established a relationship of trust and confidence with the family. By identifying the rule, however, the therapist is able to begin formulating a way to introduce a contrary rule into the family's organizational schema to make a more functional organization possible. Mother's depression can be openly acknowledged, increasing the potential for its resolution.

Although hundreds of rule possibilities may apply to a family at any given time, one rule always seems present in the more dysfunctional families—the no-talk rule. This rule is especially destructive, because it forbids any comment on family rules and, consequently, diminishes the potential for changing problematic rules. The therapist can begin to address some of the more problematic rules and demonstrate to the "no-talk" family that it can do this without falling to pieces, and, in fact, can do so with positive consequences.

As an example, assume that a particular family seems to operate with the rule, "You can interrupt anybody who is speaking except dad." The therapist could introduce a new, contrary rule, saying something like: "It is difficult for me to follow the different trains of thought I hear, as all of you seem to talk at the same time. Because of that, I'd like your help, and want to ask you to speak one at a time so that I can hear everything that each of you has to say. I believe all of you have valuable contributions to make here that will be helpful in their own way." This new rule will probably have to be reinforced before it becomes part of a new interactional pattern. Remember, the old rule has existed for a long while, and interactional patterns are not changed easily.

The following constitute examples of areas around which every family has constructed rules, and questions that can be asked to elicit family rules. How can caring be expressed in this family? How can it be received? By whom? Under what circumstances? And the same can be asked or observed regarding other emotions such as anger, hurt, and so on. How can someone let wants and needs be known in this family? Who can talk to whom, and about what? How can someone be different in this family (if that is even allowed)? When and how can a family member secure space (emotional or physical) to be alone? How can someone secure attention or concern in this family, or show or receive affirmation? How can disagreement be shown? Can anyone comment on what appear to be rules that operate in this family and create a concern for one or more members?

With many families, rules governing these areas can be determined by simply asking questions. With other families, they may need to be deduced by observing interaction. Assessment and determination of a family's operational rules can often be made by interacting with and/or observing the family. What one does not observe can be as valuable as what is directly observed. For instance, if the clinician does not observe any displays of affection despite many opportunities, a working hypothesis would be in order that a rule against displays of affection exists. A way to test this hypothesis is to ask something along the lines of, "How do you know you are cared for as a member of this family?" This question may be posed to the family as a group, or directed to a particular member. Frequently, it is best posed to the entire group, with each member having an opportunity to respond. Just asking this question will often introduce the family to a new rule that says each family member has a perception that is equally valuable. The introduction of a new and more productive rule can also initiate the process of change.

Rules can also be deduced by observing nonverbal behaviors in response to the therapist's questions. If the father, or someone else, becomes restless and seems uneasy when a particular topic or question is broached, it would be reasonable to hypothesize that a rule is being confronted or addressed that has been taboo and/or out of awareness. Or if mother and father are asked to briefly engage in an exchange about a particular issue and a flurry of acting-out by a child occurs, perhaps a family rule has been transgressed. As families become more stressed, or particular areas of their functioning become more stressed, the rules also become more evident.

Often the clinician changes family rules regardless of the particular orientation or strategy employed. When any of the following are engaged in, rules are introduced that likely replace some old, counterproductive family rules: coaching parents on management of children, regulating privacy, establishing an appropriate age hierarchy in the family, promoting open communication, eliciting feelings, providing personal feedback and interpretations to the family, and assigning tasks to be completed outside of the session. Little is done with families that either does not influence family rules or is not influenced by them. For this reason, it is extremely valuable to continually assess family rules.

≡ Family Myths

A family myth is part of the pervasive ideology of the family that evolves from the interaction of the family's rituals, roles, and rules. The therapist should comprehend this ideology, or the family's definition or framing of reality, before developing interventions. Without this understanding, there is a great risk that various interventions will be rejected by the family as not being in accord with "how it is." Naturally, when the family members are not responsive, the therapist can then project blame and define them as resistant rather than acknowledging an error in not being responsive to the family's important myths and framing of reality. For example, a family myth might be: "We are a nice family and, therefore, never openly communicate aggression." In working with this family it would be contraindicated to ask them to engage in behavior that is directly contrary to this myth. To do so would catapult the family into a contrary position regarding a component of their definition of reality, and resistant behavior would be the predictable result. Remember, myths serve the vital function of maintaining family homeostasis, or equilibrium. The therapist who prematurely and directly confronts the family's myths invites the dissolution of a relationship with them. With an understanding of these operational myths, however, the therapist can develop interventions that the family will most likely receive and respond to. To identify these myths, the therapist, in most situations, need only listen and watch the family interact, guided by the internal question: "What do these people attribute to one another, and to the family as a whole?" As therapists observe these attributions, they become aware of the prevailing myths of the family.

The process of assessing the prominent myths can also be facilitated by structured activities such as asking the family to complete sentence items. For example: "In crisis, we as a family . . . ." "As a family, we . . . ." "In this family, it is easy to . . . ." "In this family, disagreements are . . . ." and "Closeness in this family is . . . ." Another activity that can uncover family myths is to ask the family to construct an ad listing them as "a family for sale." Related techniques include asking a family to develop a symbolic family crest that conveys the essence of the family, or developing a consensus family drawing that portrays them as a group.

Along with assessing the myths about the family as a whole, it is equally important to assess myths regarding individuals in the family. Remember that myths about an individual will usually convey myths about an entire family. For example, consider this statement (by the wife) about one family member (the husband): "He is just not a good manager of finances." Statements about individuals are made in reference to one or more of the other family members, for instance, the speaker. The attribution, "He is not a good manager of finances," implies the existence of a counter or complementary myth: "but, I am (or somebody else is) a good manager of finances." In this respect, a myth about the family's organization can be deduced and used as a working hypothesis until disproved or validated by further information. In this example, it would be foolish to immediately assign financial responsibility to the husband. Knowing that the family myth functions for the family the way defenses do for the individual, it is naive to assume that the myth can be immediately confronted without preparing the family for a shift in perception and the alteration of this buffer.

To prepare the family for a shift in the myths most counterproductive to its organization and operation, the therapist must determine whether it is best to work at eliminating the family's need to maintain the myth or to gradually change the myth until the family realizes it can function without it at least as effectively as it did before. For instance, using the previous example, the therapist might help the wife feel competent enough in other areas of the family's operation so that she can more easily afford to promote the husband's financial competence, or the therapist might gradually increase the husband's competence by encouraging the wife to help him develop financial acumen. With his encouragement and direct assistance, his increasing competence is not as likely to be threatening to her, and consequently, she is less likely to sabotage the change. As the wife assists the husband in securing this new financial competence, the therapist can work with their communication styles and foster a new level of trust and understanding between them that goes beyond the issue of the husband's financial management abilities.

As you can see, the determination of family myths is vital to both developing treatment goals and establishing the path of least resistance in achieving them. The therapist who is not sensitive to family myths is probably destined to experience many apparently unexplained roadblocks during the therapeutic process and to excessively attribute resistance to the family. In this sense, the unknowing therapist may fall victim to the myth that the world is populated mostly by resistant families.

≡ Family Rituals

Assessing the ritualistic aspects of family life has long played a role in family therapy and in family therapy theory. Unfortunately, attention has been directed toward only one type of family ritual: that composed of routine interaction patterns which occur in conjunction with dysfunctional family structure and process. The type of family ritual that has been ignored and might be termed traditional is made up of activities such as holiday celebrations, birthdays, church ceremonies, and the like.

The reasons for this neglect are several, the most important being the almost complete lack of research demonstrating a connection between the problems families bring to therapy and the quality of traditional rituals. In one study, however, the disruption of traditional family ritual was found to be a principal factor in the intergenerational transmission of alcoholism (Wolin, Bennett, Noonan, & Teitelbaum, 1980). This study, as well as clinical experience, lends credence to the notion that assessing the quality of family ritual is a relevant component of family therapy.

The traditional family ritual is defined as a prescribed procedure of family interaction that involves a pattern of defined behavior which is directed toward some specific end or purpose and acquires rigidity and a sense of rightness as a result of its continuing history (Bossard & Boll, 1950). The ritual is a central component of family culture. Rituals provide intergenerational continuity and serve as developmental links in the process of family life (Schvaneveldt & Lee, 1983).

Assessing the quality of family rituals is not a complex task. When family identity seems to be well defined (meaning, when the therapist can think of a socially desirable label that describes the family), questions such as "What does the family do on your birthday?" or "What happens on Thanksgiving?" will serve to index the quality of traditional rituals. It is important for the therapist to determine who knows the rituals and how clearly the rituals can be described by family members. These questions can be directed to and answered by children as well as teenagers and adults. The most important rituals are usually spoken of first. If family identity seems well defined and yet the family members cannot describe their rituals clearly, or there does not seem to be an established routine, then the therapist should wonder whether a thorough assessment has been carried out. A negative correlation between the reported strength of rituals and a clear family identity is an indicator of inaccurate assessment.

When the family identity is not clear and a singular label cannot be applied, a more thorough process must follow. Most often, with families lacking identity, the traditional rituals cannot be described or they have lost value. Clients will often say, "We used to do_____, but over the last few years no one has been at home," or "The last time we tried to have a Thanksgiving dinner, he got drunk and pulled a knife on my sister-in-law." It is important to determine when an established ritual was abandoned. The onset of family dysfunction can be presumed to predate the abandonment of a ritual.

A second area of assessment involves the reaction of the family to its disrupted or abandoned rituals. Do the clients feel sad, resentful, or empty because this important aspect of family life is absent or awkward? Asking questions that will draw out these feelings is one way to assess the impact of lost rituals. In the process, the family can mobilize by reestablishing emotional connections and rituals. The events making up disrupted rituals are important to catalog. In the study mentioned before (Wolin et al., 1980), disrupted rituals were not found to be a factor in the intergenerational transmission of alcoholism if the family ignored the disruptive behavior of a family member and continued the ritual. Questions such as "What does this family do when she [disruption] during church or at a birthday party?" A description of events will show how the family copes with disruption of ritual and with disruption of its everyday processes. The absence of coping strategies might suggest the value of helping the family to enhance its repertoire of coping strategies.

Assessing family ritual should play some role in the overall assessment conducted by a therapist during the initial phase of therapy. Rituals are frequently related to the richness and extent of the family support network.

They provide a means of preserving family myths, especially those founded on pseudomutuality. Assessing family rituals is also a quick way to determine family roles, the structure of alliances, and subsystem boundaries. Ignoring this symbolic and binding aspect of family life can hamper the therapist's understanding of the family, and, therefore, the treatment options that may be available.

≡ Disengagement

The concept of disengagement in families was introduced by Minuchin (1974) to describe a system in which the boundaries between individuals and/or subsystems are rigid and strongly drawn. As such, the concept can be understood either as a *trait* of a family or as a *state* of current family functioning. More typically, *disengagement* is used to describe the traits of a family.

The concept is used in assessment in several ways. It is a helpful tool to use when attempting to label the interpersonal involvement of a family. Disengaged families are often silent, withdrawn, and sullen, and the members feel isolated from one another even though they may hunger for intimacy. Recognizable signs of such isolation include one-word answers to questions, ignorance of others' feelings and actions, puzzlement about why the family is in therapy, an emphasis on personal financial autonomy (teenagers working, both parents working), lack of shared family interests, low family interaction quality or quantity, lack of family secret-keeping, and other signs that communicate the absence of a strong connection between family members and a generalized concept of family.

When the clinician senses that disengagement is part of the family's usual interaction process (trait), the clarity of family identity can be questioned, or the frequent exercise and misuse of power by all family members might be assumed. Pseudomutuality, (in which claims of closeness are made, but no behavioral indicators support such a statement) may also be observed as an important family myth. When a disengaged style appears to be an unusual interaction style for a family (state), then the family may be experiencing a developmental crisis—for example, a teenager may be about to leave home and sever ties with the family.

Disengagement is an important concept in differentiating among families as to the family's level of intimacy and the strength of family members' personal identities. As with all system analysis, knowledge of the purpose served by a given level of disengagement is integral to effective treatment. For example, among families in developmental crisis (state), disengagement often serves to block channels of painful communication. Among families in which disengagement is a rigid style of organization (trait), the low self-concepts of the parental figures can be protected, the absence of a parental coalition can be maintained, and the presence of other strong coalitions can remain hidden; any number of dysfunctional patterns can be in operation. Disengagement is like a fog that distorts clinical perception, a fog that can be lifted by carefully raising a family's emotional temperature.

≡ Parentification

Parentification is a concept frequently used in the assessment of families. It is most often applied to a child who has taken on the role of parent or spouse in his or her family, although it could just as easily be used to describe any family member in another role (e.g., aunt, uncle, cousin) who assumes an adult role in a family of procreation.

The term is easy to misuse, because, in healthy family systems, we expect to see children try out adult roles. Since the parent role is the one most frequently observed by children, it is the adult role most likely to be tried out first. Naturally, therefore, we expect to see the teenage son directing the younger siblings in some chore, or the oldest daughter asking her sister and mother to quiet down during a heated discussion. Unfortunately, these natural explorations on the part of children can be mistaken for parentification.

For correct application of the label a number of conditions must exist. First and foremost is the quid-pro-quo context of inappropriate role taking. For example, a nine-year-old daughter taking charge of caring for a much younger sibling would not be parentified unless her mother or father had abdicated the parent role of primary caretaker. In this instance, parentification exists in the context of childification, in which the parent takes on some facet of the child or some other nonparent role.

A second condition involves the cost of the inappropriate role taking to all family members. The parentified child assumes role behavior and responsibility without being emotionally, intellectually, or, perhaps, physically ready to do so. As a result, stress is created, and other developmental tasks are displaced. For example, a nine-year-old who assumes the primary caretaker role for a younger sibling may not be able to spend time interacting with peers and, thus, may lose an opportunity to develop socially. The costs to other family members, mainly parents, include loss of self-esteem, because a child is seen performing what should be adult tasks, and a lowered stress coping ability, because the pressures to perform as an adult are assumed by someone else. The results of parentification should be evident throughout the system, and if there appear to be no harmful consequences, perhaps the child is in the early stages of inappropriate role taking or the role taking is incidental.

In its most severe form, parentification involves the child taking on much or most of an adult role, not just parts of it, and showing the resultant stress. The son who drops out of school and provides most of the income for his family, a behavior which the father abdicated to him along with other important aspects of the paternal role, might exemplify severe parentification. Likewise, among single-parent families in which children are asked to take on adult roles, perhaps earlier and more frequently than in dual-parent families, severe parentification would be an appropriate label when the child has taken on a number of role-related behaviors (e.g., confidant, sex partner) which are adult in nature.

In assessing parentification, the clinician pays attention to the frequency, duration, system context, and impact on child development of inappropriate role taking. Frequency and duration are assessed through the typical questions of when and how often. System context refers to how the inappropriate role taking affects all system members. Direct questions such as, "How do you feel about yourself when you see Mary Jane making the decision of which bill will be paid first?" will sometimes elicit the necessary information. With families in which parentification occurs, however, directly asking for such information may not prove successful. Inappropriate development in a child can be inferred from direct observation of the child interacting with the therapist and with family members. The presence of intense sibling rivalry, incest, or physical abuse may indicate the presence of parentification. More often, the clinician will have to infer the existence of parentification based on answers to questions unrelated to child and adult roles in the family.

OTHER ASSESSMENT CONCERNS

≡ Sexuality

Even though sexuality plays an important role in marital life, family therapists have tended to believe that sexual problems result from relationship dysfunction and to refer clients with such problems to sex therapists. We have never really decided whether to assess marital sexuality during the initial phase of therapy and how much time to devote to it. This is unfortunate because, for many couples with relationship problems, lack of sexual sophistication has given rise to those problems, and, even though treatment of those problems should not typically begin with sex therapy, exploring a couple's sexual history can be very helpful in understanding how and why current relationship dynamics came about.

Because marital therapy is not sex therapy, the procedures and questionnaires used by sex therapists are not appropriate. Most important is the therapist's communication that sex will be talked about and that the therapist is comfortable with the topic. The therapist must frankly ask questions such as, "When did you first have intercourse?" "What were the circumstances?"

"Who initiated?" "What influence did that first experience have on your relationship?" and "How frequently did you have intercourse prior to and after marriage or living together?" Using clinical terms when referring to genitalia is appropriate, and so are questions about satisfaction and orgasm. To help clients feel more comfortable, therapists often interview the couple together and then separately. Paying attention to a couple's sexual history is something a couple expects a good therapist to do.

≡ Drug Use

Alcohol and other drugs have come to be recognized as a major problem within families. A 1983 Gallup poll indicated that one-third of all respondents reported that at least one person in their family had what they regarded as a significant drug problem. Because of the pervasive nature of this problem, it is important for the clinician to know how to identify a problem, and what to do once it is recognized.

If one or more family members is troubled by another's use of drugs, it is at least an interpersonal problem which signifies a schism between two people that, if not addressed, will likely intensify antagonisms. Although acknowledging these tensions is one obvious way of identifying a problem, more objective means are available to the clinician. The Michigan Alcoholism Screening Test, or MAST (Selzer, 1971) consists of twenty-five questions that are answered with a yes or no and yields a weighted score with a demonstrated capacity for objectively identifying the intensity of a drug problem. Similarly, the MacAndrew Alcoholism Scale of the Minnesota Multiphasic Personality Inventory (MacAndrew, 1965) has forty-nine items and objectively identifies the probability of an alcohol problem existing. Both of these instruments are completed by the person with a suspected drug problem and can help to identify the problem objectively and, in this sense, lift it out of the realm of the family's perceptions. Characteristically, the family with a drug problem is pervaded by distrust, projections, and denial. For this reason, an outside and seemingly objective source can be critical in assisting the family to more productively catalog and address the problem. If family members are left only to their respective perceptions, it is most reasonable to expect tensions in the family to escalate, as reactive accusations are communicated.

Objective instruments are also available that can be completed by concerned family members to help objectify a problem. Most of these instruments are similar to the one developed by Reddy (1973), in that they consist of about twenty questions responded to by family members and have a norm-based cutoff score which is used to identify the problem's significance. As with the instruments designed for use with the person who has the suspected problem, these tools can introduce a note of scientific objectivity that replaces the highly charged emotions that have probably been rampant among family members.

In conjunction with tools such as these, the wise clinician will also have a working relationship with a chemical dependency counselor who conducts more extensive drug assessments. Such a referral source can be used when the means mentioned previously are not sufficient to facilitate a productive identification and resolution of drug-related concerns. The outcome of this outside assessment can then be integrated into the family therapy process and become part of the more complete information upon which decisions can be based.

In recent years, a great increase in understanding the concept of alcoholism as a family illness and how all members are affected by it has developed. In light of this development, the clinician should determine if either of the spouses are products of a home in which one or both parents were alcoholic, because there are specific interpersonal behaviors that can reasonably be expected from adult children of alcoholics (Wegscheider, 1981) which can be readily treated, once identified. Without treatment, these behavioral problems are likely to be transmitted to their children and to succeeding generations. In this respect, the clinician engages in truly preventive work.

The clinician should also be aware of the intervention process. This process has been described by Johnson (1973) and is designed to help the family successfully intervene and increase the potential for positive change. Although chemical dependency is a psychological/behavioral problem, physiological addiction can evolve eventually, and a major intervention is frequently then required to effect change. Johnson's widely accepted notion of an intervention consists of gathering together people who are significant to the dependent individual (family members, friends, employers, etc.) and coaching them on what to relate to the person they are concerned about, and how to relate in a fashion most likely to result in the person's making a positive decision for treatment. Without this intervention, it is most reasonable to expect that a reactive and defensive cycle of behavior will become entrenched, and that no change will occur other than problem intensification and further destruction. Interventions have now been successfully used for several years with drug problems, and it is important for these families to have clinicians available who are knowledgeable about this process.

≡ Work Problems

Although most marriage and family therapists do not receive many referrals to resolve specific work problems, work-related behaviors certainly influence family dynamics and vice versa. That work is significant to personal happiness has been long recognized, and clinicians should remain aware of this fact. Unemployment, supervisor-employee stress, dual careers, children home alone, relocations, job dissatisfaction, and retirement are all examples of work-related issues that affect families. These types of issues can provoke a variety of behaviors in families that, if not accurately related to the work issue, can seem impossible to resolve. Work also involves many "leaving-home" issues such as children going to school, adolescents to their first job, mothers to work, and fathers to new positions or jobs. Each of these changes affects the family and may exacerbate dysfunction in a family already at risk.

Work and its interaction in the family is directly related to important family constructs such as rules, roles, and morphogenic mechanisms. Rules influence the family members' perceptions of what is expected, what is appropriate, and what is possible. They have direct bearing on career selection and issues such as a homemaker taking a job outside of the home, the adolescent preferring a job or technical school to a university, and the young person yearning to move in the direction of some nontraditional occupation. Certainly, the impact of family rules will influence significantly the roles occupied by various family members and the members' subsequent sense of perceived satisfaction. Morphogenic mechanisms are those forces that promote each member of the system to develop according to complex individual needs while remaining a part of the functioning whole and not upsetting the homeostasis or equilibrium of the unit. These mechanisms affect behaviors that influence a person's career development, such as choosing a job to maintain the family name versus choosing according to individual preference (i.e., making independent choices versus choices made to satisfy others' vicarious needs).

As couples and families first present themselves, the clinician is wise to routinely assess the impact of work-related issues on the relationships represented. Often couples/families are oblivious to the subtle, but intense, impact that work-related problems have on their relationships. By inquiring about satisfaction with work and the interaction of work and marriage/family, the therapist can more clearly establish the relationship of these two important life forces. During the initial phase of therapy, there is also value in attempting to discern what can be manipulated in either the family or work environment to ameliorate troublesome behaviors. This discernment can often be used to help a husband and wife move from interpersonal conflict to a sense of cooperation and mastery over their environment.

Typically, this information will need to be extracted as part of an intake or history, because the family is often unaware of the subtle influence that work-related issues have on family dynamics. This information is particularly appropriate and important when working with families that seem unable to specifically describe the locus of their tensions. Also, the clinician can use it to begin to develop various working hypotheses about the family. For example, it is now widely accepted that alcohol problems are more frequently observed among those who work in settings characterized by frequent layoffs, long periods of unemployment, and/or frequent and long absences from the home.

≡ Stress

In the last twenty-five years, extensive research and attention has been given to the hypothesis that the stress of life's accumulated events is an important factor in the etiology of somatic and psychiatric disorders. As the body attempts to maintain a state of homeostasis or equilibrium, any life event that upsets that steady state demands adaptation. Similarly, families whose steady states are upset by life events must adapt. Holmes and Rahe (1967) have identified life events as stressors, and the response to these stressors (physiological or psychological) is labeled stress. The instrument they developed to quantify stressors is currently used by many clinicians as a routine screening tool at the point of intake.

Some have also applied these ideas to work with families. Hill (1958) advanced the ABCX family crisis model, which states that A (the stressor event) interacts with B (the family's crisis-meeting resources) which in turn interacts with C (the definition the family makes of the event), and the sequence culminates in the production of X (the crisis). McCubbin and Patterson (1982) advanced Hill's work by developing the Double ABCX model. In their model, the double A includes not only the original stressor, but also the pileup of life events experienced by the family. This work acknowledges the potential cumulative or additive effect of life events.

Recent years have brought the development of a standardized instrument called the Family Inventory of Life Events (FILE) (Olson and McCubbin, 1982). While this seventy-two-item instrument can be a valuable and quick screening tool, the clinician should be sensitive to the family's verbal presentation of various recent life events. Although the FILE can quickly ascertain the number of stressing life events experienced, it is unable to yield an understanding of the effect of these events on the family, something clinicians must determine as they ask family members about their experience of the stressors. Routinely, each family member is asked about significant events in the family's recent history; however, it is also valuable to ask them about their thoughts on how various events affected other family members. It is surprising how frequently the mother, for example, will be surprised as she hears her child vividly and accurately describe her mother's internal experience of an event. This not only provides the clinician with valuable information for assessment, but can have therapeutic value by itself. For example, this may be the first time that mother realizes anyone in her family has an understanding of her world.

Just as it is valuable to routinely assess the presence of stressors in a family, it is always appropriate to explore the presence of stressors or changes that preceded the development of a specific problem presented in therapy. This assessment is important to determine whether the problem is evidence of or is worsened by a faulty adaptation to a particular stressor. As an example, let us assume that a family's primary presenting problem is the absence of talking among family members. Assessment suggests this has been a problem for about five years, and it is also detemined that it began about the time grandfather died. It well may be that the pain, real and imagined, was projected onto others and was too intense for family members to adequately talk about. They may have resolved the problem by adopting a pattern of elective mutism among themselves. The discussion of this event in therapy may well result in a more adaptive completion of the mourning process and rekindle a sense of concern and connection long absent. Intervention of this sort effectively serves to dislodge the family from the problematic solution (that it originally perceived as a problem). In this sense, the solution to the problem became the problem, which is often the case in a family's attempts to adapt to various stressors.

For these reasons, the clinician is wise to routinely inquire about recent stressors to determine the existence of a correlation between stressors and onset of problems. Not doing so prevents important information from surfacing and may significantly delay responsiveness to treatment.

≡ Sexual or Physical Abuse

Sexual and physical abuse are frequently found to coexist. Their long-term destructive effects are obvious. Although relationship problems sometimes promote and maintain these problems, these behaviors themselves often confound and entrench family difficulties. Therefore, astute therapists should be sensitive to detecting abuse in order to ensure that they provide appropriate treatment.

To determine if sexual/physical abuse is present in the family, therapists need to be comfortable enough with their own values and attitudes to approach families in a matter-of-fact, but sensitive, fashion. Calm and direct questioning of the family can provide an atmosphere of permission absent from the family before therapy. Such an approach communicates to the family members that the therapist is not intimidated by abuse problems, and it also establishes a counter-rule to the no-talk rule frequently observed in these families. The therapist needs to convey a sense of competence and strength, while simultaneously establishing the important counter-rule.

Finkelhor (1979) has stated, based upon his research, that one percent of all females are sexually abused by a father or stepfather. Also, certain characteristics of families, such as the presence of an alcoholic parent, seem to increase this probability. Research has identified other correlates to the existence of sexual and physical abuse in families, and the presence of any of them should increase the therapist's need to inquire about this type of abuse. In addition to the presence of an alcoholic parent, other indicators are as follows: the family with poor mother-daughter connections/bonds; a mother who is very dependent either psychologically or physically as the result of illness or accident; a father who appears to be very controlling and possessive of his daughter(s); an acting-out adolescent girl engaging in sexual promiscuity or suicidal gestures who is a frequent runaway or drug abuser; or a child who appears to be very overresponsible and parentified in the family context. Although it would be inappropriate to assume that physical/sexual abuse is present in any family manifesting any of these indicators, it seems just as inappropriate to neglect further exploration when they are present.

If sexual abuse is disclosed, therapists must be aware of their legal responsibility to report such information to the proper authorities. All states now have reporting laws, and although there is some variance about who is to be reported to, there are strict consequences for the professional who has access to information about abuse and does not follow through with a report (see Chapter 4). Being aware of the very low incidence of falsely reported incest by children, therapists must not delude themselves into thinking that child-reported abuse is just a prank. Remember, not reporting and allowing abuse to continue is no favor to the victim or the family.

Having made a report, the therapist must be concerned about promoting the best interests of the children and ensuring their safety. Although geographic variance exists as to the handling of these incidents, the recent trend is that children are not immediately removed from the house. Professionals now recognize that removal of the child tends to have the following effects: intensify the child's sense of guilt, decrease the potential for strengthening the mother-daughter bond that is so crucial to preventing future incidents, increase the likelihood of the daughter's being scapegoated and excluded from the family, promote the likelihood of the father's seducing the mother into an alliance with him, and create the problem of having to find a good placement for the child in the meantime. Instead, fathers are usually asked to leave the home while the investigation proceeds. During this period, the family will be in need of much support and assistance, along with intensive treatment. The nature of the treatment required is beyond the scope of this section, but therapists are reminded of the importance of exploring the presence of these behaviors in the family, and then acting, if they hope to be of help to these people. Granted, it can appear to be very disruptive and temporarily destructive to the family, and likely will be, but without disruption, the hope for productive change is minimal.

ASSESSMENT TOOLS

≡ Self-Report Tests

As the field of marriage and family therapy has developed, objective instruments for assessing and cataloging problems have evolved. These instruments are employed for both research and clinical purposes. Although their use in gathering research data is obvious, their use in clinical practice seems less well understood.

As couples and families enter therapy, they are frequently confused by the morass of accumulated emotions they have experienced. Unless issues to be addressed are specified, the therapy can become as fragmented as the clients' emotions appear to be. The advantages of using self-report instruments with couples or families include: (1) they can help to objectify and organize the treatment effort while establishing an atmosphere of purposeful direction to replace family chaos; (2) they provide family members an opportunity to systematically understand what the other members' concerns are (perhaps for the first time, the confusing cloud of emotionality is somewhat dispelled), and, (3) individuals are provided with the opportunity to self-disclose through paper and pencil rather than their usual method, which has failed. Frequently, people will find it easier to respond to a checklist of potential problems or specified questions than to describe their concerns verbally. After reviewing a list of marital problems, such as those found in the Marital Diagnostic Inventory (Navran, 1973), couples often report a new perception of their difficulties as they discover that they checked relatively few of the many possible problems. This insight, by itself, can often have great therapeutic value, not to mention the specificity now available to the spouses and the clinician.

The clinician can derive benefits from self-report tests as well. As with any journey, therapy can be expedited with the aid of a map. By using self-report instruments, the clinician can organize the interview data and construct a valuable cognitive map which describes the type and nature of problems being presented. Without this map, the therapeutic journey can become a series of rambling, unsuccessful side trips, unproductive for all involved. Further, gathering this type of information at the outset facilitates evaluation of treatment outcomes; many clinicians administer the same instruments at a later phase in therapy to get feedback on the nature and extent of client changes.

Although many objective instruments are available, clinicians are wise to review them and select the ones most consonant with their style and practice; test publishers are eager to share information about their available instruments. Also, reviewing books such as Straus and Brown's (1978) *Family Measurement Techniques* can prove valuable. Although the marriage and family therapy literature of the 1970s is replete with polemics about this or that correct method or instrument for measuring presenting problems, clinicians do best to select those tools that best fit their practice.

In selecting instrumentation, keep in mind the relative complexity of intervening with the family unit as compared to the individual. Ackerman (1958), almost three decades ago, stated that a complete family assessment should take into account the individual family members, roles, the marital dyad, the family as a group, and family members' interrelationships. Fortunately, objective instruments now exist with which to assess these areas, should the clinician so choose.

≡ Using Metaphorical Language

The utilization of metaphorical conversation, or speaking of one object or phenomenon as though it were another, can be a very important assessment procedure. Recognizing that most people are in therapy as a result of distress or duress, and that most people are not comfortable talking about their problems, it is important to make the experience as natural and comfortable as possible. The use of metaphors is one effective way of doing this.

By developing an understanding of the contexts people come from, and of how they formulate and describe their problems, the therapist can get valuable clues as to how to develop metaphorical ways of framing notions that will facilitate understanding. For example, a couple who owns a farm and are concerned about the absence of vitality in their marital relationship, despite their best attempts to "get the other to do what they want," may respond well to a metaphor. The therapist could compare marital relationships to the crops they rely upon for income:

> You know, a marriage is very similar to your work. You are unable to get crops to grow by going into the fields and pulling at them or demanding them to grow. Instead what you need to do is carefully plant them and ensure that appropriate fertilizer and other essentials such as water are available. A relationship does not prosper by someone pulling at it or being demanding either. Like your crops, the relationship needs to be tended to and cared for by each of you. How about if we were to begin by each of you identifying what would serve to help you feel better and to promote your well-being and the relationship.

With the husband or father who is a mechanic by trade and appears to be relatively uninvolved in his family life, the following might be an effective metaphorical way of communicating:

> In working with cars, you know that the absence of routine maintenance will result in major problems. If routine tune-ups, lubrication, and oil changes are not performed, there will be major problems eventually. Relationships are very similar. Without routine attention and care, even-

tually there will be major problems. Let's brainstorm for a few minutes and determine what kind of things you might be able to do in this family that are like routine preventive maintenance in your business.

Metaphorical language cannot only be very effective in drawing people into the therapeutic process; it also frequently encourages them to develop further metaphors from their own experience to describe problems. Whatever the clinician does to enhance people's capacity for understanding and communicating their experience is likely to be helpful, and the use of metaphors is one way of doing so. In this regard, the assessment process is facilitated while the clients' potential for learning about their perceptions is increased. Also, metaphors can provide a channel of communication that places clients at ease and helps them to understand their difficulties in ways that, many times, make more sense.

≡ Circular Questioning

The technique of circular questioning, used as an assessment tool, has the unique value of placing clients in a metaposition, outside of the system they are currently embroiled in. As the family members listen to another member respond to circular questioning, they also may learn for the first time what this member's perceptions of the family operation are.

Circular questioning also tends to elicit information in a nonthreatening way and especially can help clients who have difficulty expressing themselves directly. For instance, rather than asking someone who is reluctant to respond, such as an adolescent, the sister can be asked to respond as she believes her adolescent brother would. While this provides the information requested, at least from the sister's perspective, it also serves as a stimulus for the brother to respond by correcting his sister or agreeing with her.

O'Brian and Bruggen (1985) have offered a helpful means of categorizing types of circular questioning. One of the types they identify focuses on relationships in the family and is divided into questions that are about two other people in the family and those that are about people in relation to events in family life. For instance, in reference to two other people in the family, the therapist may ask one member, "How do your mother and sister get along?" or "How do your mother and father show that they care for one another?" Regarding people in relation to events in family life, the therapist might ask, "When your sister says she's not going to bed at night, what might your mother do?" or "When your wife drinks as you just described, what will your daughter do? What will she be feeling?"

O'Brian and Bruggen suggest another category of circular questioning designed to help people engage in ranking behavior. Ranking can occur in relation to actual or hypothetical circumstances. For instance, a question about an actual circumstance might be, "Who does the most disciplining of you, your mother or your father?" or "Among your brother and sisters, who would you say is most disturbed by this situation?" Ranking questions that refer to hypothetical situations might take a form such as this: "When all of your children have grown and gone, who will have the most contact with you, then who, and so on?" or "Let's assume the drinking doesn't change; who will be most disturbed and in what ways, and then who?"

Another category of circular questioning relates to time. These questions may focus on a specific event or project forward or backward in time. Examples of questions regarding a specific event are "How was John different before mother's death?" or "How do you think Suzy felt differently before mom and dad's divorce?" Examples that project forward or backward in time are "How do you remember things being between mom and dad six months ago? How do you think your mother was different then?" or "What do you think Suzy will be most fearful of one year from now if things don't change?"

The last category identifies questioning which refers specifically to a person who does not answer questions presented. This may be someone present who chooses not to respond or someone not present in the session. For instance: "If John answered the question I just asked him as honestly as he could, what would he say?" or "If Jack were here today, what do you believe he would say about that?"

Circular questioning can be a powerful tool to employ during the assessment phase of therapy and at other times, also. Besides generating valuable information for the therapist, it can also begin to expose the family to itself in new ways that promote new understanding. Further, it can speed the gathering of information, overcoming the problems of various family members' feeling too shy to talk and of family rules that do not allow family members to directly share the information another member offers about them in response to circular questioning.

≡≡3≡ TEACHING

INTRODUCTION

Teaching is a most important therapist skill that is not talked about by authors of family therapy texts or by supervisors. The reasons for this omission are several, the primary one being that teaching is not perceived by mental health professionals, especially by those seeking to enhance the public image of their profession, as a therapeutic activity. In addition, most therapists are not trained to label, as teaching, those aspects of therapy which involve showing a client how to do something or instructing a family in the process of the family's interaction. Hopefully, however, family therapy clients do learn in the context of therapy; such learning is the result of a teaching process, no matter how dissimilar that process is to academic instruction.

Teaching, in the context of therapy, is an individualized process that consists of showing clients how to do something that will improve family functioning or relating information that will change client attitudes in order to motivate family members to take new actions. The important elements of successful teaching in therapy are (1) a well-defined ability to know when to switch into a teaching mode (recognizing the teaching moment), (2) awareness of what it is that clients need to be taught and what they can learn in the context of a single therapy session or part of a session, (3) the ability to demonstrate what the clients are to learn and to clearly present new ideas when attitude change is in order, and (4) well-developed skills in providing actual instruction. This chapter covers the most common teaching needs of the family therapist. The three elements in successful teaching will be described and applied in each chapter section.

PROCEDURE

The key to success in teaching is to use a systematic training procedure, following three basic steps. First, a rationale for learning the skill is presented to the clients. Second, the skill is demonstrated. Third, the clients practice and receive feedback while they perform the skill.

The first step, stating the rationale, is designed to explain what the skill is, why it is important to learn, and how the skill will benefit the client. People learn more easily and cooperate more when they understand the purpose of what they are to learn and what the payoffs will be. For example, eye contact is commonly taught as an attending skill to listening. The rationale for this subskill might be explained as follows:

> Good eye contact is designed to communicate that the listener is paying attention to what is being said so that the speaker feels attended to. When good eye contact is present, a speaker usually does not need to get angry or resort to some other attention-getting strategy to make sure that the listener pays attention. Good eye contact consists of looking in the pupil of another's eye and moving back and forth from eye to eye while the other speaks.

Typically, clients will want to discuss the rationale, especially for complex skills. Such discussions are important because misconceptions can be clarified when they occur rather than at some later time when they may result in client failure. In addition, during the discussions, the therapist can usually model using the skill while the discussion occurs and enhance the validity of the rationale in the process. Once clients understand why the skill is important and what the payoffs will be, the skill needs to be demonstrated.

Cotherapy teams have an advantage when modeling skills for clients. Unfortunately, most therapists work alone and often must ask a client to help with the demonstration, unless the skill does not require the participation of more than one person. A creative and efficient therapist will use a demonstration in which a client helps as an opportunity to do more than model a skill. For example, in demonstrating how family members can talk together without interrupting and how signals are to be used in asking for the floor, the therapist might ask the family member who interrupts the most frequently to play the role of someone who is speaking and who relinquishes that role when signaled by the therapist.

However, the most important factor to keep in mind when demonstrating is that the modeling must accurately depict what clients are to learn. A demonstration of good listening, for instance, should show good listening and not something else. That means you, the therapist, must know how to perform the skill you are asking clients to learn. In addition, the modeling should have a direct application to the problems confronting the family in therapy. For example, in demonstrating the time-out procedure for parents with young children, the behavior attended to during the demonstration should be one that the children in the family perform at home. The more clients can identify with the situation depicted in the demonstration, the more likely they are to value learning the new skill and to understand how they can use it at home in everyday life.

An excellent follow-up to a demonstration is to ask clients what they saw you doing. Spending a few minutes in discussion at this point helps clarify the specific behaviors clients are to copy and allows you to clear up misunderstandings about what is and is not to be done.

The last stage in the teaching procedure is to have clients practice the skill and receive feedback on their performance. It is at this point in teaching that therapists most often make a mistake. Usually, the mistake is to demonstrate a skill and then ask the family or couple to continue the discussion that preceeded the switch from therapy to teaching, while one family member attempts to practice. Not surprisingly, most clients have difficulty performing the skill well, because the situation used for practice is emotionally charged. Always have clients first practice a skill in a low-threat situation. For example, when teaching listening to a married couple, assign them a nonrelationship issue to discuss in their first attempt to practice listening. As the spouses' skills improve, the topics can proceed from positive relationship issues, to minor problems in their marriage, and then to the larger issues. As a result of controlling the content of their discussion, the spouses can concentrate on learning instead of defending or attacking.

Another important task in this phase is to let clients know that they are performing well, or at least in close approximation to what has been demonstrated. The easiest way to give clients this type of feedback is to say, "Good" or "That's it" or some other short phrase of reinforcement. When clients are first learning, they need this type of feedback fairly frequently (say, three times over a three-minute period). Once they know they are doing well, you can give the feedback every five minutes, and then reduce it to occur only after a practice segment has ended. When clients do not do well, stop them after a short time. Often, a second demonstration is in order, or perhaps one of the above factors that inhibit learning (i.e., topic too emotionally charged) is active and is affecting their ability to concentrate.

Once a therapist knows this three-step strategy of teaching, the steps can be applied to many different skills that clients need to help them interact better and to feel successful in therapy.

RECOGNIZING THE TEACHING MOMENT

One of the most important teaching skills is recognizing when to leave the therapy mode and to enter the teaching mode. Unfortunately no one guideline exists to help the therapist decide; several factors must be considered.

The presence of high emotionality indicates that the teaching mode is not appropriate. For example, when a wife finally explodes at her husband about his drinking, an appropriate response on the part of the therapist is to make sure her message gets through. An attempt to teach appropriate listening to the husband while he is in the midst of guilt or defensiveness will fail. Likewise, when a client is sobbing, therapist instruction in the skill of self-disclosure will be unsuccessful, and the client may even be offended at the therapist's inappropriate attempt to intellectualize and abstract. The emotional intensity of a situation, therefore, is one factor therapists must take into account when considering whether to teach or do therapy.

Another factor is the amount of time in a session that can be devoted to teaching. Skills training and attitude change do not occur without a substantial investment of time on the part of the therapist. A comprehensive skills training program, for example, that is designed to include both listening and self-disclosure skills for married couples requires approximately eighteen hours of instruction time when the instruction is carried out in a small group format. Less time is needed when both skills are taught to individual couples, although the amount of practice time needed is not significantly less. As a result, most therapists teach a component of the more generic skills. Rather than teaching empathic responding, most therapists teach eye contact or nonverbal attending. Teaching even these skills takes time, however, and it is important that enough time be devoted to their instruction that clients will be able to learn and practice the skills. Inadequately developed skills that are the product of too little time spent in explanation or practice are harmful, because clients will not successfully use them in every day life and may also resist future instruction. Allocate enough time in a session to fully teach what is appropriate.

A third factor pertains to the need of the client to know or learn the new skill. Teaching is most beneficial when the client experiences a real need to know. For example, suppose a wife is disclosing her feelings about her troubles to her husband and comes to an abrupt halt, followed by a complaint that her husband is not paying attention, and his reaction is not defensiveness, but puzzlement. In that moment, the therapist could, over a two- or three-minute span, teach him a nonverbal attending skill, and he would be able to practice the skill in a situation requiring it. Such moments abound over the course of a therapy session. Husbands and wives interrupt one another, children get noisy, and spouses distract and intellectualize; all of these incidents in therapy can be dealt with by teaching what clients need to know at the time they need to know it.

Another excellent time to teach is when a session gets dull. When you feel bored, it is likely that your clients are also feeling bored to some degree. Switching to teaching can be a change welcomed by all concerned. The difficulty is deciding what to teach. Naturally, what is taught is most helpful if it pertains to the interaction prior to the switch to teaching. If you cannot think of anything appropriate, a transition statement that specifies a change of topic is necessary to help the clients switch their attention from their previous interaction to learning something not associated with it.

LISTENING

Most often, listening is taught to married couples, family members, and individual clients who consistently break the basic rules of effective listening. To assess what to change, the therapist must know these basic rules:

Nonverbal Rules
1. Maintain eye contact with speaker.
2. Use head nods visible to the speaker to comunicate understanding.

Verbal Rules
1. The intent of a listener's statements or questions should be to clarify the speaker's message, not to change the topic or gain control of the speaker role. The listener role should be that of a follower.

Therapists often attempt to teach reflective listening to clients. This attempt commonly fails because not enough time is allocated to the teaching process. When listening is taught in the context of therapy, it is far better to change nonverbal behavior and to limit a listener's responses to those designed to clarify speaker messages than to attempt to teach reflective listening.

The steps in the teaching process are as follows:

1. Discuss

   Discuss why eye contact is important.

   Discuss why it is important for the listener to follow the speaker's lead instead of guiding the speaker's awareness.

2. Demonstrate

   Demonstrate eye contact (it may also be helpful to show clients what their current behavior looks like).

3. Practice

   Ask the client to copy you while listening to the spouse or other family member.

   Reward the client, if appropriate, and give feedback.

   If the client cannot do what is asked, change the topic of discussion, as it may be too threatening for skills training.

   Practice until the skill is understood and performed well.

   In future sessions, ask about the client's use of the skill and watch for its appropriate use in session.

SELF-DISCLOSURE

Of the two basic interpersonal communication skills, the speaking skill is not as well developed as the listening skill. The concepts of *I messages* and *ownership of feelings* are more like buzzwords than descriptions of concrete skills. Good self-disclosure consists of talking about yourself and your feelings and thoughts about yourself in relation to some event or situation. Opinions are not part of self-disclosure, nor are interpretations of others' actions.

Rules of Effective Self-Disclosure
1. Speak about yourself, how you view yourself, how you contribute to relationship problems, how another's actions are a problem for you, how you react to another's actions.
2. Avoid statements or words that will interfere with getting a message through to the listener. Words such as *always* and *never* should be used with great care.

The primary difficulty in teaching self-disclosure is that many therapists emphasize the disclosure of feelings, and, unfortunately, clients (especially men) do not know the difference between thoughts and feelings. As a result, clients do not feel successful even when they try to be more feeling centered and disclosing. A better tactic is to tell clients to talk about themselves, how they contribute to relationship problems, and how others' actions are a problem. Ordinarily, the client will talk about feelings in the process of answering these questions without becoming confused about whether they are talking about feelings. In addition, the therapist's use of phrases such as "disclose your feelings" and "own your feelings" may stimulate additional arguments in the family or marriage when one spouse accuses another person of not being feeling oriented.

The steps in the teaching process are as follows:

1. Discuss

   Discuss why self-disclosure is important in a family or marriage. Through self-disclosure the important problems are identified, intimacy begins and grows, and personal burdens are shared.

2. Demonstrate

   Therapists who demonstrate self-disclosure should take care not to be too analytical about themselves or too intimate in their demonstration.

   The topic should pertain to the important issues being dealt with by a family.

   The demonstration should include the person most likely to be undisturbed by the therapist's intimacy.

3. Practice

Ask the couple to continue their topic of discussion while using the new skill, but only if the skill is still applicable.

If the clients cannot do what is asked, make sure they understand the rules of effective self-disclosure.

If they do understand and still cannot stop themselves from accusing, interpreting, and intellectualizing, change the topic to one that is less emotionally laden.

FEELING AWARENESS

It is common today to encounter clinical problems that are partially based on deficient awareness of feelings and/or communication of feelings. Men and teenagers, it seems, are prone to not feeling or, at least, not disclosing their feelings at home.

Rather than first attempting to understand what role nonfeeling plays in maintaining homeostasis, a therapist might attempt instead to increase feeling awareness and expression by stating that feelings are OK and coaching clients to respond to questions such as, "How do you feel?" Typically, the supposedly unfeeling client stumbles and mumbles until the therapist gives up and relationship homeostasis is retained.

Lack of feeling awareness/communication among relationship members is not always due to a simple lack of skill. The cold, withdrawn husband, for example, may be highly expressive about sports; elaborate technical schemes; or sophisticated business plans. In a similar manner, a withdrawn teenager may be highly disclosing in a nonverbal way with friends. In such cases, nonexpression may be an attempt to maintain interpersonal power in the family. Where nonexpression appears to be stable across contexts and relationships, however, a lack of skill may be the reason.

Whether inexpressiveness is a power play or the result of a real skill deficit, the therapeutic strategy consists of first encouraging talk, not the disclosure of feelings per se. Clients feel awkward and resist when asked to label their feelings in therapy with questions such as, "How do you feel?" They will cooperate, however, if asked to simply describe some important part of their day or some discovery they have made about themselves. Some prompting and questioning may be required to keep the client talking. Most importantly, however, the client's spouse needs to pay attention to the talk, but differently than in the past. To learn how the client's partner has attended in the past, a role play will prove very informative, or the partner can be questioned.

When clients are able to talk about themselves, their reactions, and thoughts, a didactic discussion of feelings and their function in relationships becomes possible. Feelings in relationships serve two functions. First, disclosing feelings creates the opportunity to build trust, and then intimacy, between partners. Second, familiarity with emotional reactions adds zest, color, and meaning to personal life. Disclosing feelings in relationships also lets a partner know whether a request for change or a request for the familiar is important or unimportant. Feelings acquaint spouses with the vitality of their relationship, and feelings help them appreciate each other. When told of these purposes that the communication of feelings serves, spouses are usually motivated to express more feelings to each other.

PROBLEM SOLVING

Considerable research has been conducted on effective procedures for teaching problem solving in the context of marital and premarital intervention. Unfortunately, little of that body of knowledge is used by family therapists, because therapy is not viewed as an opportunity for clients to learn complex, new skills. Problem solving is one such skill that builds on clients' competence at listening and self-disclosing.

Problem solving is taught as a process of steps used to help couples find solutions that work. The process itself does not generate solutions, but it does provide a structure couples can use to identify, try out, and evaluate their own solutions. The steps of a typical problem-solving model include:

1. Defining the problem or complaint,
2. Expressing how each partner contributes to the problem,
3. Brainstorming alternative solutions,
4. Selecting and contracting a solution, and
5. Evaluating the outcome.

The therapist's role in teaching problem solving is more like that of a guide than a model, because many of the steps do not require new behavior that must be carefully shaped. In the first step, defining the problem, spouses use effective self-disclosure and listening skills. Problem statements become less threatening and the usual attention-grabbers, such as yelling, become unnecessary. After a period of time spent discussing the problem or issue, and when the speaker can state the problem clearly, the couple should be told to move to the next step of the process in which they each discuss how they contribute to the problem. These statements tend to be surprisingly open, because the task's structure forces each partner to admit helping to cause the problem. Usually, very little therapist intervention is needed other than to make sure both spouses feel listened-to by their partner.

In step three, the process takes on a playful tone, with the partners listing alternative solutions without evaluating any proposed solution. Evaluating solutions as they are being listed tends to stifle creativity. The therapist's role is to encourage creative solutions and make sure the structure of the problem-solving model is adhered to. In the next step, the alternate solutions are evaluated, and one workable solution is discussed. In this step, the partners make an agreement or contract that details how the solution is to be implemented. The final step, evaluating the solution, is completed after a trial period of several days, weeks, or months, depending on the frequency of the problem and the nature of the solution.

Of the different types of training, problem solving is perhaps the easiest. It usually follows more basic training in communication skills after which couples possess a skill foundation that helps minimize bickering and passive-aggressive behavior. The role of the therapist is not so demanding, because although the skills are more complex, they involve behavior in which most people have engaged. The essential ingredient to effective problem-solving training is to limit the size of the issues that couples attempt to resolve until they have been successful in dealing with minor problems.

PARENTING

Many of the problems presented by families in therapy involve the skill of the parental subsystem in carrying out the parenting role. As a result, the family therapist is often called upon to show adults how to parent. Unfortunately, many therapists do not have a detailed knowledge of basic parenting skills, and all too often, therapists' recommendations are not understood, or they are forgotten, because time is not taken to teach clients how to carry them out. Following are descriptions of the procedures used to teach the most frequently needed parenting skills.

≡ Rule Setting

All parents need to set rules, and all children struggle to discover what they are. Most of the parents seen in therapy use the yell-and-hit method simply because they know of no other. Because so much emotional energy is required to carry out the yell-and-hit and because this sanction is so severe, it is not used consistently. It can result in withdrawn and acting-out children and abusive parents sentenced by the courts to family therapy. These parents need to learn a method of setting rules that is low-cost in terms of emotional energy expended, allows for increasingly severe consequences for a child's noncompliance, and promotes consistent use.

One such method is the three-step procedure for disciplining young children that is taught in most of the currently popular parenting programs. The first step in this method is for the parent to explain what the child cannot do and then suggest an attractive alternative. For example, if a child is drawing on the wall with crayons for the first time, the parent should stop the child, look him or her directly in the eye, and calmly state, "You cannot use your crayons on the wall, but you may draw on paper." The second time the problem occurs, the parent should restate the rule and give a consequence for its violation. Following the same example, the parent should stop the child, look him or her in the eye, and state, "You may not draw on the wall with crayons and if you do it again, I'll put you in time-out." The third time, the parent restates the rule and imposes the consequence without hesitation.

For very young children (between three and five years of age), the entire three-step sequence may need to be repeated if several days or so pass between episodes, because they may not be able to remember the rule. Older children (six through eighteen years of age) respond to time-out or to the loss of privileges ranging from watching favorite television shows, visits to and from friends, to receiving an allowance, using the family car, and meals. Of utmost importance is consistency. Encourage parents to keep a few rules consistently and let the rest slide.

To teach this method, the therapist must know the rule-setting sequence and be able to cite examples, the best of which are based on incidents provided by the parent(s). The teaching procedure consists of first stating the rationale for changing the parents' current rule-setting method. The rationale for the three-step method is as follows:

1. The current method used by the parents does not work, and it costs too much in emotional terms.
2. The three-step method will encourage them to enforce rules more consistently.
3. Children will learn that they can and cannot do.

Second, the three-step procedure is described, using examples, and discussed in order to make sure the parents understand the rationale and how to implement the procedure. Finally, the parents are asked to role-play, using the procedure, in the therapy session. When they are able to go through it without prompting, they are asked to use the method once before the next session and to note other times they could have used it. The next session should begin with their report of how things went and when they could have used the method but did not, followed by role play using the three-step method in the situations they used the yell-and-hit method. Next, the parents should be asked to use the new procedure more often during the next week, but only in situations they think are appropriate for the three-step method. Over a few weeks, parents will stop using the yell-and-hit method except in a few situations, and a new skill can be attempted.

≡ Time-Out

Time-out is a child management procedure that all parents need to learn, even if they are not active child abusers. The procedure is very simple, and it is effective after a child learns that the parents will use it and use it fairly. The difficulty parents have in punishing children is that corporal punishment instills guilt in the parent and fear in the child; thus, physical punishment does not encourage parents to consistently enforce rules. Time-out helps parents establish consistency, and consistency provides children with the boundaries they need to feel secure.

Time-out should be used in the three-step procedure described previously. The idea of time-out is to move a child from a high-stimulation situation to one that is low in stimulation. The time-out place should remain the same; good examples include a chair in a corner, a dimly lit hallway, or a stairway. When step three of the rule-keeping procedure is required, the child is sent or led to the place and instructed to remain there for a short period of time. The length of time the child should remain in time-out is guided by the child's age. Two-year-olds should spend no longer than two minutes in time-out, three-year-olds three minutes, and so on, until the child is seven or eight, when ten minutes can be designated. While the child is in time-out, reading or any other activity should not be allowed; the experience is supposed to be boring. If the child does not voluntarily stay sitting or standing and remain in the time-out place, the parent must physically keep the child there.

In teaching this method of child control, the mistake most often made by therapists is in not requiring the parent to role-play placing the child in time-out during the therapy session. Instead, many therapists merely describe how to institute the procedure and then check up on its success the following week. For effective learning, the parent must be required to practice by sending a child to time-out under supervision. If asked, children will gladly cooperate by misbehaving and allowing themselves to be sent to time-out.

≣4≣ THERAPY PROCESS PROCEDURES

INTRODUCTION

Once the initial phase of therapy has been completed, it is time to undertake the middle phase in which most of the work takes place (Barnard & Corrales, 1979). Many of the procedures used in family therapy have been developed for use in this phase, and very few of them will be effective unless several conditions are met. First, procedures work best when a relationship has been established in which the client perceives the therapist as competent and authoritative. Second, unless the therapist has diagnosed the family in terms of its systemic functioning, implementing a procedure may be a waste of time or even lead to deterioration. Lastly, the therapist must have won, for the moment, the battle for structure, and act as the leader in the consulting room. As long as these conditions are met, the procedures described in this chapter may bring about the conditions in which change can occur.

MANAGING COMMUNICATION WITHIN SESSION

≡ Ending Chitchat

Chitchat, or small talk, is an important part of all therapy, but especially of family therapy. Upon first meeting, individuals use chitchat as a way to get acquainted. After we come to know another person, we use chitchat as a preface to further interaction. Within a group of people, such as a client group, however, small talk is more likely to dominate verbal interaction unless the group is moved toward its tasks. Small talk can inhibit the progress of therapy unless it is controlled.

Controlling small talk means initiating it at the beginning of a session and then quickly communicating that the session is beginning through a transitional or directive statement. The question, "Well, how did things go this week?" often serves to indicate the end of small talk and the beginning of the session. Initial interviews often begin with the phrase, "How can I help you?" or "What problems are you experiencing?" or a more provocative question, "What do you want to change in your marriage [family]?" An alternative is to remain standing with the family during small talk and then sit down to indicate that small talk is at an end. Whatever signal is used, marking the transition from small talk to the task of therapy is the therapist's responsibility. Attention to this procedural detail will often result in a greater sense of movement by the therapist and greater confidence on the part of the clients that their therapist has the ability to be helpful.

≡ Everyone Speaks at Once

Many authors have commented on dealing with this difficulty. It is a problem most often seen in first sessions, usually as a result of family anxiety. The therapist can often help dispel this anxiety by taking care to direct statements and questions to specific family members, rather than to the entire group. If the family persists, a request from the therapist that all speak for themselves will usually suffice.

When these efforts do not produce the desired result, the therapist can safely assume that a homeostatic communication pattern is used by the family to prevent message sending and receiving, de-skill the therapist, or block the effects of therapy. In this situation, some small object (a pencil, magazine, hat, etc.) can be used as a symbol granting permission to speak, and a family member can speak only while holding the object. As with all rule making in therapy, the therapist needs to explain the rule and why it is being imposed. Such a statement might be:

Hold it! I cannot hear or even think when everyone speaks at once. Let's try using this pencil to slow things down and agree to a rule. The rule is that the only person who can speak besides me is the one holding the pencil. Whenever I ask a family to follow this rule, we always go through a short time when it seems clumsy, but after a while it will be easy. My job will be to make sure the rule is kept. Now, John, you were saying . . . [gives the pencil to John].

When this procedure is first instituted, the family may react in several ways. Younger children are especially likely to break the rule. Parents, not the therapist, should restate the rule to the child, and then the person who was interrupted should be directed by the parents (prompted by the therapist) to continue speaking. When an adult breaks the rule, the therapist should immediately intervene by saying, "Stop!" or some similar remark, along with a visible nonverbal gesture (raising arms) that stops all speaking. When all speaking has stopped, the rule should be restated, and the interrupted person encouraged to continue talking. Again, the therapist's role is to maintain the rule.

Another way for a family to react is for someone other than the speaker to complain that the pencil is being hogged or kept too long. In this instance, the rule must be kept, and the therapist can designate the family member who wants to speak to go next *after* the person holding the pencil has finished. When the speaker has voluntarily finished, the family member feeling slighted can be encouraged by the therapist to disclose any irritation and then continue with another message.

When all attempts to keep the rule fail, there is a final option. More experienced therapists correctly view such maneuvers by a family as a battle for structure, and they will refuse to engage. Not participating in a battle means simply leaving the session and telling the family that when they are ready to follow the rule they can ask the therapist to rejoin them. Such a contingency is best delivered without showing frustration or irritation with the family, although these feelings will most certainly be present. Some therapists are rather lenient about keeping the rule, but many choose to implement this last option very quickly once the rule has been described to the family and been broken. Allowing a family to win a battle for structure blocks therapy, leads to the therapist's developing a dislike for a family, and contributes to therapist burnout.

The purpose of imposing and keeping the rule is to help the family members learn that they can allow each other to speak their minds without falling apart. The new rule imposed by the therapist also establishes a new norm of interaction that can enhance communication and mobilize family resources to better deal with problems.

≡ No One Speaks

Silent, nondisclosing families and their members are among the most frustrating clients encountered in clinical practice. By definition, such a communication pattern may serve to repress interaction, feelings, and even thoughts. To cope with such clients, clinicians often join the family system by withdrawing and eventually terminating therapy.

To avoid this trap, careful diagnosis must determine whether silence is the result of not knowing what to do in therapy, of a skill deficit, or of maintaining homeostasis. Two good diagnostic indicators are whether the family has been in therapy before and whether its members are adquate in other areas of their lives. For example, if the occupational status of the adults requires adequate interpersonal skills, or if the children have friends with whom they are close, an absence of family communication is most likely not due to lack of skill. In the case of the family that has not been in therapy, the family members may need to be instructed that therapy is the place where talking about their thoughts and feelings toward one another is expected. If the adults function at an overall low level, and the children appear to be isolated even from one another, the family members may simply not know how to express themselves. When communication skills are absent, the clinician can have the most impact on the family by teaching. When silence serves to maintain homeostasis, however, other tactics are best used.

Therapists often assume that the client family is colluding to maintain a family secret, and then design treatment to make the secret public. Unfortunately, although maintaining a secret may have initially stimulated the family's silence, long-term silence virtually requires family members to become numb; the effect is that, in fact they have nothing to say to each other or to the therapist.

Whether the family is hiding a secret or has become numb, the procedure to open communication is the same; initially, the therapist must do the talking for the family. The difficult question is: What should be said? In the initial interview, all families, even those described as low-disclosing, will divulge information about their lives and, certainly, information about the critical incidents bringing them into therapy. Through this information gathering, the therapist can come to an understanding of the different stresses and concerns experienced by each family member. This understanding is partly the product of the information about the family environment provided by the family, but it mostly depends on the mind of the therapist, who must imagine the feelings and thoughts of each family member based on their roles. For example, the spouse of an unfaithful partner typically feels betrayed, embarrassed, hurt, and angry, and the parent of a runaway child usually feels angry, embarrassed, guilty, manipulated, taken for granted, and confused. In silent families, these feelings are not communicated and often not even perceived, so it is up to the therapist to state them as if expressed by the family members themselves. The therapist's job in this situation is to break the family rule of silence by guessing what the feelings and thoughts of its members are and stating them openly.

An important part of this procedure is how the thoughts and feelings are delivered. If a child's thoughts and feelings are the focus, the therapist needs to take the role of that child, perhaps standing or kneeling beside the child while speaking for him or her. Adults can be dealt with in the same way. Speaking for any family member, however, calls for high-order empathy. A therapist must take on the role of the individual member spoken for, and, for the sake of credibility, try to make statements that accurately reflect that member's viewpoint, even if guessed at.

If the therapist's guesses are correct, a family member may feel understood and take the risky step of saying, "Yes, that's it!" The therapist's instruction immediately following is to say, "Go on, tell us more," and a few words will come stumbling out. If no one reacts to the member's statement and the interaction dies, the therapist can use the same empathic skill and the same creative guessing to understand other family members' reactions to the disclosure and state them openly.

Speaking for a family is a lot of work, but with prompting and encouragement, a therapist can, over a number of sessions, gradually fade out of the speaking role as the family members become more aware of their thoughts and feelings, and as they come to trust that disclosure will not result in crisis.

≡ Clients Ramble On and On

Clients who talk on and on, seemingly ignorant of the rules of human interaction, often pose a real barrier to progress in therapy. Whether the family conspires to encourage the rambling or whether such behavior is engaged in out of habit or due to anxiety, it is the therapist's task to intervene. Most often, a comment that communicates the therapist's feelings of impatience or irritation will change the client's behavior, at least for one session. When other family members are also frustrated by parent or sibling rambling, they can be encouraged to express their own needs to talk and their feelings of not being able to. The situation in which nothing is effective is the most trying and leads therapists to have thoughts of letting the person talk until spent and to consider paradoxical strategies of encouraging more rambling. However, a different approach deserves mention, because it works so well.

First, note that the chief difficulty of interacting with nonstop ramblers is how to gain the floor without awkwardly grabbing it. Most people are socialized not to interrupt or speak while someone else is talking; we hesitate to barge in on someone's discourse in order to avoid feeling guilty and insensitive. As therapists, we fear that we may model an awkward interruption for our clients. As a result of not knowing how to interrupt and gain the floor, we permit our clients to continue unchecked. However, a way to interrupt without awkwardness and then take the floor is available.

The procedure consists of two steps which are based on the idea that even the most stubborn of ramblers will stop to listen to a simple reflection or summary of their comments. Consequently, the first step consists of verbally or nonverbally capturing the client's attention and then summarizing the client's thoughts and feelings. Then, before the client has a chance to reply or continue talking, the therapist takes command of the floor by asking a question directed toward another family member or by directing the verbal interaction toward some other topic (the second step). For example, suppose a rambling client, distracted from describing a presenting problem, begins to talk about a pet. The therapist might interrupt with, "Let me see if I understand. You were puzzled by Misty's need to always be next to you." Then without pausing for even an instant, the therapist would direct a question to another family member, "John, how would you like the family to change?" The first step permits the therapist to interupt smoothly and legitimately, and to communicate caring and understanding while setting the stage for the opportunity to take control of the conversation. The second step redirects the conversation to whatever the therapist chooses. Even though it may need to be implemented over and over again, this procedure helps manage rambling clients by making the therapist less hesitant to interrupt with a method of gaining the floor that is less crude, abrupt, and offensive than the usual.

≡ Family Members Speak for One Another

Commonly, the communication patterns of families seeking help prohibit some members from speaking for themselves. Those speaking for others believe that everything is fine, while, in reality, those being spoken for are angry and feel ignored or stifled. When such a problem exists, it is the therapist's job to enable all family members to speak for themselves.

Right from the start of therapy, it is most effective to institute the rule that people are to speak for no one but themselves. In the initial interview, for example, parents may try to speak for children or one spouse for another. When this occurs, the therapist needs to react immediately by saying something like, "I'd like Sally to say what she thinks," rather than permitting the violation to continue. If after several such interruptions, the family does not comply, the therapist must address the problem directly by saying, "I'm having difficulty learning what Sally thinks about this, so I'd like her to explain it in her own way. I would also like us to agree on a general rule that no one speaks for anyone else unless I ask you to. That way, I think we will all learn more from each other."

Refusing to accommodate a family's usual communication pattern is a powerful, destabilizing tactic. It may take several sessions for those who have been silent to open up.

≡ Clients Speak to Therapist, Not Each Other

Because spouses have difficulty communicating and come to therapy to have their problems solved, more often than not they will direct remarks to the therapist rather than to their partner. This pattern of interaction is common in the initial session.

In later sessions, the therapist who retains the role of listener for both spouses becomes triangled between them. Instead of increasing disclosure, trust, and intimacy between the married partners, session time is spent developing these interpersonal dynamics between the therapist and each spouse. Although some relationship development between the therapist and the spouses is necessary, the emphasis of marital therapy should remain on the partners' relationship, and early in therapy the partners need to be encouraged to speak to one another.

There are several ways to encourage clients to speak directly to one another without expressly directing them to do so. The first way is to phrase requests specifying who is to be spoken to, for example, "Tell John how you reacted to that"; a client will typically follow through and converse with their partner. If not, a nonverbal gesture pointing to their partner will usually spur compliance. If the client still addresses the therapist, the therapist should repeat the two strategies just mentioned, break eye contact with the spouse who is to speak, and look at the other spouse. If these maneuvers do not work, the therapist can explain that in marital therapy the partners should feel free to interact with one another, and that frequently they will be directed to do so.

A more direct approach to encouraging spouses to interact is to seat them directly facing one another. As with all requests, compliance is more likely if the spouses understand what they are to do and why. For example, if the therapist wants to get a sample of their communication style when discussing a negative issue, the following might be said:

> I'd like to get an idea of how the two of you talk together on this issue. Turn your chairs around so you are directly facing one another. Marsha, I'd like you to bring up the topic as you usually would . . .

Or, in another situation when the therapist wants to make sure the partners are attending to one another so that an important message gets through:

> I want to emphasize the importance of that message. Turn your chairs around to directly face each other. Now, say the same thing again.

More often than not, spouses need direction from the therapist to interact with one another in therapy, in part because our social custom is to include others in conversation. The participant responsible for changing this norm is the therapist.

≡ Clients Take Potshots at Each Other

Therapy is a new experience for many couples and families, and they tend to be on their best behavior initially. As anxiety decreases, however,

_ eir *at home* interaction style will probably emerge. It usually includes put-downs, confrontations, and a host of other interpersonal attacks and defenses that fit under the rubric of verbal potshots. As a family becomes more comfortable in therapy, these behaviors tend to be displayed more frequently in session, if the therapist so permits.

Verbal potshots are short, quickly delivered, hit-and-run statements designed to gain some momentary interpersonal advantage. Name calling, using words such as *never* and *always* in an accusation, and assigning motive (for example, "You just want me to give in so you'll feel superior") are examples of potshots. If the therapist does not take steps to prevent such behavior and does not intervene when potshots first appear, then clients may rightly assume that they are to behave in session just as they do at home. If therapy is to be successful, however, clients must learn to behave differently.

As has been often stated in family therapy texts, the purpose of family therapy is to change the way a family system functions. By definition then, clinicians are successful in this task depending on whether they permit a family to maintain homeostasis. Therapy sessions are the time and place to initiate new behavior that changes homeostasis.

Stopping verbal potshots is a straightforward procedure consisting of two steps. The first consists of acting—doing something immediately to stop interaction. That means keeping careful tabs on what clients are saying and acting quickly once a potshot is delivered (before the receiver of the attack has a chance to respond). It also means that clinicians must overcome their socialization not to interrupt others' conversation. There is nothing wrong with barging into an interaction with the statement, "Hold it, that was a potshot, not allowed in here." Hand and arm waving, standing up, and stretching one's legs out are nonverbal ways to accomplish the same task of stopping or distracting clients from continuing to behave as they have in the past.

Once the interaction is stopped, the next task is to direct the attacker to restate feelings and thoughts in a constructive manner, and for the therapist to discuss why such behavior is harmful to the communication process. To elicit a restatement, the therapist might say, "You definitely have some strong feelings about . . . . What do you mean to say?" The client (a spouse, for example) will usually explain the message to the therapist. Through the use of empathy skills, the therapist can help change the message to one that is less accusative, more revealing, and helpful instead of harmful. Then, the therapist can direct the client to state the new message to the other spouse, along with the statement, "What you said initially was a potshot. The next time you want to get back at her [him], say what you mean so the message can get through. Potshots only confuse issues, make her [him] defensive, and your message does not get through." If the therapist gives consistent attention to stopping dysfunctional communication when it occurs in session, clients will learn to stop themselves at home, and the homeostatic patterns of communication they have developed over time hopefully will evolve into new and more functional patterns.

≡ Clarifying Clients' Unclear Labels

Couples and families often come to therapy with difficulties that, in part, are the product of misused or undefined labels. Concepts such as independence, dependence, trust, temper, depression, and many more contribute to communication breakdowns among intimate relationship members.

Throughout therapy, one important task that belongs to the therapist is to help clients communicate with one another more clearly and avoid the traps created by undefined labels. As in any relationship, the therapeutic relationship develops along with the acceptance of certain concepts and labels used to describe important feeling states. Unless these labels are mutually understood by all participants in therapy, the prospect of change may be limited because the lexicon of communication symbols is not shared.

In the first session, especially, the therapist must listen very carefully to the labels clients use. For example, if a wife describes her desire for more independence in her marriage, she should be asked to clarify what the label *independence* means to her. When clients state they are afraid of their partner or another family member, their fear needs to be defined. Another example involves the label *trust*. One spouse might say, "I just don't trust her anymore." Responding to these labels, the therapist might ask, "What do you mean by . . .?"

When asked to clarify their labels, clients are often confused by the therapist's request for a definition. If clients comply and explain the label, communication is aided. When clients balk, remain confused at the request, or define the label with a circular definition (for example, to trust is to trust), either they do not know what they mean or they are maintaining a dysfunctional pattern in the family system. When clients do not know what they mean, conjoint session time or an individual session can be devoted to clarifying the label. When the undefined label plays an integral role in maintaining system dysfunction, the same steps can be taken, but clarification may not be forthcoming. The clinician may first need to change other aspects of family system operation so that a client can perceive an advantage to clarifying an important label.

≡ Guiding Client Attention

An important aspect of any form of therapy is the management of client attention. Clients suffering from depression, for instance, focus attention on their feelings and thoughts of gloom, whereas clients with paranoid ideation focus attention on the behavior and intentions of others to confirm their suspicions of betrayal or harm. Similarly, family members tend to blame an identified patient (IP) for family problems and focus their attention on the IP in an attempt to confirm their beliefs.

In addition to other interventions, it is the therapist's job to direct clients' attention toward other aspects of their lives. Consequently, during the therapy session, a depressed client might be asked to list positive events experienced the previous day. The client who accomplishes this task is led, at least for a short time not to dwell on or attend to negative thoughts and feelings. In another case, the clinician may attempt to reframe or relabel IP symptoms to reorient family attention away from the IP toward the family system itself. A good argument can be made that all types of effective therapy consist mainly of contriving ways to manage client attention from minute to minute.

Managing client attention requires that the therapist not only maintain an awareness of what clients are attending to from second to second, but also structure sessions so that clients can easily follow the topics of discussion. The therapist must provide an adequate transition between topics. For example, in the following interaction the therapist does not provide the needed transition:

Therapist: "John, you seemed to get uncomfortable when Alice became angry just a minute ago."

John: "Yeah, well she gets pretty hot sometimes, and I'm never sure what she's going to do."

Therapist: "Sometimes you are afraid of her."

John: "Yeah."

Therapist: "How was anger expressed in your family?"

John: "What?"

In this situation, the therapist may have had a very salient point to make, but the change in topic from John's feelings to his family of origin was so radical that John got lost. Had the therapist provided a transitional phrase connecting the two topics, John's attention probably would have been directed toward answering the question instead of asking what it was.

The same interaction, with a transition statement, would appear as follows:

Therapist: "John, you seemed to get uncomfortable when Alice became angry just a minute ago."

John: "Yeah, well, she gets pretty hot sometimes, and I'm never sure what she's going to do."

Therapist: "When she gets angry you get scared of her."

John: "Yeah."

Therapist: *"I'd like to sidestep for a moment here to find out where you learned to react to anger that way.* How was anger expressed in your family?"

While we may question the effectiveness of such a shift in topic, the inclusion of the transition statement by the therapist efficiently guides John's attention in a direction that the therapist believes will prove beneficial.

Providing transitions is also important at other times. The need for transition words between presession chitchat and the beginning of a session is familiar to all therapists. Moving from a homework report to the main session task also requires a transition. Clients also profit from transition statements (summaries) that tie sessions together. As a result of paying attention to transitions, therapy flows more smoothly, transactions between therapist and client are less ragged, and the potential for understanding is enhanced.

≡ Encouraging Family Grief

Unresolved grief sometimes serves as an emotional brake to the development of a family and its individual members. The family that does not successfully mourn losses often stops growing from the time the losses occur. Losses may come in the form of physical death; loss of an ideal (for example, a feminine son instead of an idealized athlete); divorce or other loss of a significant relationship; not receiving an important promotion (in the case of a parent); not completing an academic goal such as graduation; or a child marrying someone other than the parents had desired. Therapists need to remember that losses comprise many human experiences besides the obvious one, death.

Significant losses can be determined in a number of ways. One way is to pay attention when a family identifies a loss as a significant time in the family's life. Another way is to inquire during intake about significant losses/ disappointments the family encountered in the last twelve months. Research by Holmes and Rahe (1967) has documented the importance of this period, although losses earlier than this may also be very significant. When a family identifies a particular problem as having begun at a certain time, the wise therapist will inquire whether significant losses occurred at about that time, because unresolved grief may have provoked the family's presenting problem. For instance, problematic drug use by a family member often closely relates to a significant death in the family. Remember that a family member's death will result in the loss of several important roles that the dead member had filled and the disruption of rules that the dead family member had helped to maintain. Also, death accentuates issues for survivors that relate to belongingness and separateness, or closeness and distance in relationships. These all constitute important accommodations the family must make that can provoke faulty adaptations culminating in a multitude of family problems. For example, death may result in the family's pulling together more strongly just at the time an adolescent member is in the process of leaving the family (as part of the differentiation process resulting in rebellious behavior by the teenager).

In general, the more open the family, the more effective the family members are at coping with losses and the accompanying grief. Lewis, Beavers, Gosset, and Phillips (1976) have examined the family's potential for dealing with death, finding that the families most open to discussing death are also the ones most functional in other ways. Consequently, the therapist's task consists of identifying important losses that have not been successfully resolved by the family, or by particular members, and then facilitating resolution. Norman Paul (1967) refers to the process of facilitating belated resolution as *operational mourning*. According to Paul, this process consists of the therapist's inviting exposure and expression of feelings attached to the loss by repeated and direct inquiries. It is important to recognize that the family may have developed fairly rigid and dysfunctional rules governing the expression of this affect that will need to be penetrated and changed.

Similarly, Bowen (1976) has identified the importance of using direct words to communicate a new comfort level to the family in discussing death (such as *death*, *die*, and *bury*, instead of *passed on*, *deceased*, or *expired*). Using empathic relating demonstrates to the family how to talk about sensitive issues attached to losses. It also desensitizes death issues and shows that they can be confronted directly without the family's falling apart. Having all family members present during the process of operational mourning helps them learn how to relate more empathically, and reap the immediate benefit of sharing the experience. The immediate experience can also be used to promote family discussions about how family members might help each other deal with the present loss and with future losses. Last, the belated resolution of losses can help the family establish permission, rules, and procedures for adapting to the inevitable.

MANAGING ANXIETY WITHIN THE SESSION

≡ Raising and Lowering Anxiety

Typically, the therapist's and family members' experience of anxiety fluctuates during the course of a session. A certain look on a wife's face provokes anxiety for her husband; older sister's hand on little sister's knee lowers anxiety; the adolescent stands and rushes out the door, which raises anxiety for the therapist; dad's talk of hopelessness and suicide intensifies anxiety for all family members. Each person's experience of anxiety can be affected by the various behaviors and interactional sequences present in the session. Because anxiety occurs on an ongoing basis, most often out of the control of the clinician, situations will arise requiring the clinician to appropriately manage anxiety-inducing cues.

When a family seems to have become complacent about the change process, without sufficient anxiety to provoke further change, the clinician has a variety of options for stimulating anxiety. The number of options is limited only by the clinician's perceptions of the family's organization and creativity. For example, the clinician might refer to "the family that was seen a few months ago" that resembles this family: "They were saying things exactly as you folks are now, and seemed to be feeling the same things. It seemed that just when they thought they had things fairly well under control, all hell broke loose. You know, the similarities between you now, and that family just before the intensification of problems are spooky. I've seen it before, too. It seems too bad, when folks have made the kinds of advances you have up to this point." This type of comparision often piques the family's curiosity and anxiety enough to induce the family to explore possible ways to secure further change and maintain change effected already.

Sometimes, however, a particular subsystem of a family is so firmly entrenched in its attributions to, and perceptions of, a family member, that change seems highly unlikely. In the absence of anxiety that might stimulate change, the subsystem's perceptions have created a self-righteous sense of indignation and anger. For example, recently, a family was seen by one of the authors that contained two parents and two daughters, ages six and ten. The parents presented the problem as that of the ten-year-old's being obstinate and unmanageable. It was quickly determined that as obstinate as the ten-year-old was, the parents were at least as obstinately critical. These two crucial components of this apparently endless cycle acted as both cause and effect, and at least one needed to be altered if there was to be hope for change.

At one point in conversation, the parents mentioned how similar the ten-year-old was to the husband's brother, who had been extremely depressed at various times in his life. The parents made it evident that they had been very helpful and responsive to this brother and prided themselves on their contribution to his "recovery." This similarity was explored and became the focal point for increasing productive anxiety to stimulate change. The similarities between the brother and daughter were amplified by the therapist until the daughter was viewed as being as much depressed as "obstinate." The obstinance that was present was related to depression, and a plan was devised with the parents to help them be as helpful to their daughter as they had been to the husband's brother. The concern, or anxiety, for the daughter becoming as depressed as the brother was sufficient to motivate the parents to change their obstinately critical way of relating to their daughter. As suspected, the parents' more moderate and compassionate way of relating to the daughter was quickly met by her becoming much more cooperative and caring. A benevolent cycle had developed between the parents and daughter, replacing the old destructive one.

Just as there are times when it is valuable to intensify the experience of anxiety, there are also times when it needs to be mediated in order to open a pathway for change. One of the authors recalls working in a clinic at a time when a local newspaper carried an article by a psychoanalyst that declared that playing with matches by five- and six-year-olds suggested a multitude of future problems for these youngsters. During the next several weeks, the clinic was flooded with intakes of five- and six-year-olds who had been caught playing with matches. Predictably, the parents of these children were experiencing intense anxiety secondary to a concern that their child was doomed to an adulthood ravaged by a variety of unknown mental disorders. A crucial task in working with these parents was to attempt to ameliorate their anxiety and normalize the curiosity of their children. With few exceptions, there was considerable evidence that the children were simply responding in a curious fashion to fire as an interesting phenomenon in their world. If the parental anxiety had not been mediated, it is reasonable to assume that their overresponsiveness and concern could have increased the likelihood of problems being observed in these children as they grew and developed.

As was true in the previous example, providing information to replace the destructive notions that current behavior is based upon frequently reduces anxiety. In another case, the couple who presented concern for the wife's being unable to experience an orgasm in spite of penetration for at least three minutes responded very quickly to the correction of their notion that three minutes should be enough. Clinicians often waste valuable time searching the depths for the etiology of a problem, only to stumble across the discovery that all that was needed was a simple piece of information to replace current erroneous information. Frequently, information that normalizes and reframes, or places behavior or an experience in a different perspective, is what the family is most in need of in order to moderate anxiety. While this sort of intervention is not what makes for dramatic case presentations, it is often what can be most helpful to concerned families.

≡ Inducing a Crisis

There may be times in working with a family when the clients' anxiety levels have fallen too low, and the uneasiness or tension that can be so important to stimulating change is lost. At these times, the therapist might consider inducing a crisis by amplifying a particular deviation already present or manipulating the family affect so that dynamic tension is rekindled (Minuchin, 1974).

Amplifying a deviation can take a variety of forms. Assume that a couple has been seen for some time and appears to have settled into a complacent pattern. The therapist may choose to identify a particular piece of behavior in their relationship and then amplify it. If the husband, for example, makes a comment to his wife that could be interpreted as demeaning or discounting in nature, either in its content or the style used in delivering it, the therapist could amplify this deviation by saying to the wife: "How do you feel about his saying that or the way in which he said it? I can really appreciate that if I was in your shoes, I would probably feel hurt, but also angry too." This form of amplification involves the therapist's assuming what Zuk (1981) refers to as the side-taking function, by aligning with the wife to support her in addressing the husband's discounting style. The husband's behavior may otherwise go unnoticed by the wife, and the therapist's effort to amplify the deviation serves to promote interaction that can result in change. As Zuk indicates, though, the therapist must be sensitive to the dynamics of the clients' relationship. For instance, in the example offered, it would be wise for the therapist to create some sense of alliance with the husband to serve as a buffer or shock absorber against his possible perception of being ganged up on by the therapist and wife. If the appropriate alliance is present, the husband will not become unduly defensive and will be able to productively address the concern identified.

Manipulating the family affect is another means of promoting a productive crisis within a family. This refers to changing the affect a family member attaches to a particular experience and assumes that a change in affect will also promote a change in behavior. Take, for example, a family with a mother, father, and some children, including one adolescent who has been disruptive and problematic. Assume the adolescent's disruptiveness is correlated with the parents' apparent inability to activate some authority and set limits with contingencies identified for transgression of these limits. The adolescent makes a comment that is disrespectful of the parents, perhaps even a blatant put-down. The therapist asks for the parents' feelings about the comment, and the parents report: "Well, I don't know for sure, but I imagine it's his right. You know, I'm just not certain what to say."

This would be a time when the therapist may move to manipulate the affect by making a comment such as:

> I'll tell you, I'd be mad as hell if he said that to me. I don't believe you deserve that, as I think about how concerned and helpful you've attempted to be. Perhaps the problem is that you've been too damned concerned and understanding. I definitely believe that you are deserving of more respect than that comment suggests.

The effort is then continued to promote the parents' having some righteous indignation to the point that they begin to assert themselves as parents and executives in the family. The effort is made to initiate new behavior by creating a crisis or, as in this example, manipulating the affect that the parents are attaching to their son's behavior.

Therapists who are not comfortable enough to periodically promote a crisis could be destined to many episodes of apparent lethargy and no change by the families they are involved with. In using this procedure, though, it is important for therapists to be candid regarding their motivation and ensure that it is not to satisfy their own feelings of frustration with the family. If there is any reason for doubt, the therapist should probably discuss this possibility with a supervisor or colleague.

≡ Defusing a Crisis

Just as there are times when therapy can benefit from the therapist's inducing a crisis, at other times, productive therapy dictates that a crisis be defused. To defuse a crisis, therapists have the option of using themselves to create an intentional triangle or referring the family to its past crises to activate resources that helped them in earlier circumstances. To illustrate the first option, assume, for example, that the family enters a session in crisis. As the family comes into the room, at least one family member is overtly and intensely irate with another member. The angry family member is shouting, blaming, and spouting accusatory indictments and appears intent on continuing these expressions. The other family member gets defensive, but that member's efforts do little more than further incite the angry person. A therapist can intervene at this juncture and begin to defuse the crisis by becoming triangled in the relationship.

One way of doing this is to say, "I can see and hear that you are really upset about this and I need to hear it, but I need you to slow down so I can fully understand, and I need you [said to the one who is the target of the anger] to just be quiet for a short while. All right, let's go ahead. Please tell me what this anger is about." The therapist then encourages the angry member to speak directly to the therapist and to quit attempting to get any further response from the person the anger is directed at. During this time, the angry member should receive the therapist's complete attention, along with periodic efforts by the therapist to clarify and ensure that this member feels understood.

Once the emotion has been stated, the therapist can turn to the member who is the target of the anger and ask for a response to what the target has just heard. During this time, if the angry member attempts to interrupt, the therapist can say: "I know you're really angry, but I need to hear this completely. I assure you that I'll be coming back to you in just a minute. I want to make sure I understand all this, and I'm sure you want me to." By preventing them from directly addressing one another, the therapist allows the angry member an opportunity to ventilate and have the affirming experience of being heard and understood at the same time. Intercepting the direct interaction between these two members also prevents things from escalating to the point of destruction.

The interaction is continued in this fashion, with the therapist actively introduced as the third point in the communication triangle. Direct interaction between the partners at these times often activates old destructive patterns of defensive relating. As a more manageable level of affect is achieved, the family members can be encouraged to interact directly with one another.

Returning the family to their past is another means of defusing a crisis. Assume a family comes into a session in great distress over the fact that father has just been informed that he has been laid off from his job. After acknowledging the nature of the crisis and understanding the family's distress, the therapist might implement this procedure by saying, "I realize this may be the most upsetting thing to fall on you folks in some time, if not ever, but what was the last situation that was almost this distressing?"

This intervention does a couple of important things to defuse a crisis and enable the family to be more proactive. First, when confronted with a crisis, people tend to be so consumed with its immediacy that they lose sight of the fact that they have encountered and survived other crises. Asking this question reminds family members that they have encountered other tough times, and they are still here to experience this current crisis. It is important not to ask them about the last crisis that was "this bad," because the current crisis always seems to be the worst. Acknowledge at this point by asking them about the last situation that was "almost this distressing". Second, once the last situation is identified, ask the following sort of questions: "What did you find helpful that time? What did you do? Who was helpful to you then?" These questions help the therapist to determine what resources the family has activated in the past that it may use once again.

In addition to confronting crises, therapists can take the preventive measure of predicting crises ahead of time. This encourages the family to do some preventive planning prior to being consumed by the crisis, and increases the therapist's credibility in the family's eyes once the crisis does come. For instance, as a family resolves a problem, they might be asked to predict what the next crisis might be and to talk about ways to resolve it. The therapist may also simply predict that some crisis is about to occur, based on the family's level of readiness for difficulties. The prediction can help the family identify the next crisis in terms of the family's "readiness," rather than perceive it as a fault or weakness of the family.

≡ Assessing When to Confront

Confrontation is a valuable though potentially explosive, technique when used appropriately. Just as nuclear power has tremendous positive value to humankind, yet equally destructive power, confrontation has the same potential in relation to family therapy. In general, confrontation has its greatest therapeutic value after the development of a relationship that provides for adequate shock-absorbing quality. If confrontation is engaged in without evident caring and commitment, it can be perceived as caustic or designed solely to injure. Certainly, confrontation is a procedure that could provoke termination by the family, but, perhaps more importantly, create an impression for the family that all therapy is more injurious than it is helpful so that they never seek help.

Gerald Zuk (1981) has written the most explicitly about confrontation with his description of the process of side-taking by the therapist. Zuk goes so far as to say that families will not allow the therapist not to take sides, and even if the therapist attempts to remain neutral, the family will perceive the therapist to be taking sides, anyway. Consequently, Zuk encourages the therapist to accept side-taking as a natural part of the therapeutic process and to use the process of confrontation to produce the greatest therapeutic value. Cautions about this process have to do with becoming too predictable and the need to monitor the structure of the family to avoid injuring clients. For instance, always confronting the adolescent member of a family could encourage the adolescent to develop a rigidly organized set of defenses to the therapist that prove impenetrable later on. Or confronting a mother who feels her husband and children have ganged up on her could lead her to terminate therapy.

The therapist can apply confrontation to a variety of issues such as: family members' definitions or labels attached to a person or behavior; communication styles that are counterproductive; patterns of responding to others in a fashion that curtails productive relating; unwillingness to compromise; and reluctance to acknowledge another's point of view. The confrontation can take the form of a direct confrontation between therapist and another person, or between therapist and subsystem of the family, such as the parents. The confrontation can also be packaged in a variety of ways, depending on the therapist's perception of the situation. For instance, the confrontation may be presented in a teasing and playful fashion in the case of a client who seems to be tenuously engaged in therapy, or it may be offered as speculation that really does not demand a response—for example, "You know, I think you probably do that just to get the type of reaction I saw you get. Makes sense to me." Naturally, the confrontation can also be very direct and truly confrontational. Confrontations that are more direct may be necessary to underscore the seriousness of whatever is at issue.

They might also be the most appropriate way to get a message across simply to a client.

The use of confrontation is probably one technique in the therapeutic arsenal that is most reflective of the art, rather than science, of therapy. The therapist must assess a family's circumstances at the time of the confrontation, as well as its appropriateness and likely consequences, before implementing it. The therapist who does not do this is likely to find that many families terminate without explanation.

≡ Confronting Clients

As defined by the lay person, confrontation is a hostile, unpleasant, demeaning, and anxiety-provoking experience that is best avoided. These feelings result from confrontations in relationships and encounters that produce frustration, irritation, and anger.

These same feelings are often experienced by therapists toward clients. In family therapy, such feelings are good indications that the therapist is becoming enmeshed in a family system. If a therapist acts out these feelings, the result is often client hostility, appointment no-shows, or at the least a "stuck" case. Talking with a colleague helps in disengaging from the family and reestablishing a therapist role. There are times, however, when therapists need to confront clients with their feelings. When fees are not paid or when therapy is not taken seriously by court-referred clients, for example, feelings are created that need to be communicated.

The essence of good therapy is confrontation, but of a different sort. Therapeutic confrontation involves close examination of client's patterns, or feedback about client behavior, followed by a statement of what is not obvious or is not easily revealed. For example, in listening to a daughter describe her relationship with her mother and her lack of sorrow when the mother died, a confronting statement might be, "It doesn't sound to me like you two were very close to begin with," or "In talking about her, you seem to be stifling a lot of strong feelings." These two statements are confrontational, but are usually stated in a manner that is not offensive or demeaning. The crucial difference between offensive versus therapeutic confrontation lies in the therapist's tone of voice and intent to be helpful.

≡ Client Abruptly Leaves Session

On occasions, a member of the client unit will abruptly leave a session amidst an intense display of emotion. In view of the intensity of affect often observed among family members, the therapist should not be surprised by this occurrence. It often provides important new observational data about family organization and operation. Who appears to be most affected by the display of behavior? What do the remaining members say and do in response? Who are the ones activated to comfort, distract, or behave in some other way at this time? Answers to such questions can provide information to the therapist that may otherwise be uobtainable. This is also a time to determine what family members want to do to make their response differ from their predictable one, and what prevents them from doing so.

The therapist may also want to use this situation to effect change by moderating a family's usual pattern of not allowing a member to be angry, for example, or by securing some individual space, or even by encouraging a family to react in a way that provides too much space and evidences an absence of responsiveness to the member's affect. The therapist can also negotiate with the remaining family members the decision of who will go to retrieve the departed family member or to comfort them, whatever is therapeutically dictated. Whether the member returns to that session or does not return until the next one, it is usually valuable to process with the entire family what provoked the display and the way the members responded.

During such a crisis, young therapists will often have to control their impulse to assume responsibility and do something that the family member could benefit from doing, such as going out to retrieve the departed member. To become overly responsible for the family in such an instance could deprive the family of a valuable learning experience.

EFFECTING BEHAVIOR CHANGE

≡ **Describing a Behavioral Pattern**

In attempting to promote behavioral specificity with clients, modeling the process of describing a behavioral pattern for them can be valuable. For instance, assume that whenever a wife says to the husband, "There you go again, will you grow up!" he becomes withdrawn and appears to retreat. Then she escalates her attack, and he responds with greater withdrawal, and so on. To describe this pattern, based upon observing it more than once, a therapist might say,

> Have you two noticed that when Joan says 'there you go again, will you grow up,' Larry, you become quiet and begin to drop your eye contact and appear to become inattentive. Joan, his actions seem to promote more anger and frustration from you, along with an increase in verbal statements that seem to get more of the same withdrawal and

inattention from you, Larry. I have observed this on more than one occasion, and I'm wondering about its usefulness to your relationship.

They are then invited to comment on this observation. The question at the end of the statement supposes that the patterns exist. It also serves to imply that the pattern ought to change.

The value of describing behavioral patterns lies not only in helping clients become aware of behaviors that would otherwise remain automatic, but also in introducing the possibility that the identified patterns may evolve into new treatment goals (see "Establishing Therapeutic Goals" in Chapter 2). Although the therapy may already have more general goals, an identified pattern can facilitate the achievement of a larger goal (such as improving communication effectiveness to diminish a sense of not being valued by one another) or it may become a specific minigoal by itself.

Patterns are often more easily detected early in treatment, before the therapist has become so familiar with a couple or family that everyone is oblivious to reoccurring behaviors. In this regard, reviewing audio or video-tapes of sessions can be particularly valuable, as can inviting a colleague in for a consultation session with the specific identified purpose of observing, and then guessing at what might constitute patterns.

Clients' responses to reports of behavioral patterns by a therapist will frequently cause them to use those very patterns. For instance, with the example used before, it would not be surprising to observe Joan beginning to attack Larry as he becomes withdrawn, and so on. The astute therapist will be sensitive to this behavior pattern and be prepared to use it to confirm the presence and strength of the pattern. Once the behavior pattern has been identified, it is valuable to have each client identify how the other might help that client stop contributing to the pattern in order to prevent its occurrence, and then rehearsing these proposed behaviors in session. For example, Joan might ask Larry to tell her when he is feeling accused/attacked by her by simply saying so or combining his report with some apparently absurd behavior, such as pointing his finger at her and crossing his eyes. By incorporating the absurd component to this reporting process, the sharpness of the exchange can be minimized while still conveying the necessary information. Continuing with the example, Joan might report to Larry when she perceives him withdrawing and appearing to become inattentive and accompany this statement by holding her hand to her mouth like a megaphone and saying, "Am I being received over there?"

≡ Reframing Symptoms

Reframing, as the procedure is called in the context of therapy, is designed to change the clients' views of their problems. Family therapists especially recognize that clients' definitions of their problems often perpetuate those problems by narrowing the range of possible solutions. Consequently, a first step in changing how clients act often consists of attempting to reframe symptoms and problems so new solutions can be tried out.

The reframing message itself can consist of a mere comment or a lengthy statement. When the therapist merely comments to reframe symptoms or problems, there is little attempt to persuade clients of the veracity of the reframe. For example, if the identified patient (IP) is a child who has run away from home, the therapist might comment to the parents, "You know, I think he's trying to help you two get your marriage together by giving you something to talk about." Such a comment may be influential in helping the child's parents begin to address their own marital relationship issues. If the spouses ignore or miss the point of the therapist's comment, which is likely, they will maintain their view of the family's problems and restrict solutions to those already proven ineffective.

Reframing is most successful when the therapist attempts to actively persuade family members that the reframe is not only a plausible reconceptualization of their problems, but also more accurate than their old conception. To take this persuasive tack, time must be invested in discussing the reframe, and evidence documenting the new conception must be cited. To continue with the example, the therapist might begin in the same manner:

> You know, I think he's trying to help you two get your marriage together by giving you something to talk about. I recall you saying that before John threatened to run away, the family, and especially your marriage, was dull and no one seemed to feel cared for. I know it may seem difficult to believe that John's behavior has the goal of bringing you two together, but consider what has happened. You two are spending more time together than either of you can remember, and the focus of your attention is inside the family. Also, consider the effects of his actions on the other kids. They are spending more time at home and they are quarreling less. I'm sure you can think of other ways that John has been helpful to the family. Let's take some time to discuss this different way of viewing John's behavior.

The intent of both the comment and the more lengthy statement is to introduce an alternative view to the one currently used by family members to understand their situation. Instead of casting John as the bad child, he is praised, and a rationale is presented from some others aspect of family life—in this case, the marriage—to become the focus of treatment. As in all persuasive statements, the reframe message takes a specific form and has specific content. First, the IP's behavior is labeled. Then, the actions of all family members in response to IP behavior and the reactions of other family members to those responses are specified. The positive contribution of IP behavior to family functioning is described, and last, the cyclical nature of these responses is introduced. Such a complicated statement can be composed on the spur of the moment during a session, but more effective reframing statements are figured out between sessions when proper attention can be given to detail. The therapist's intent in delivering a reframe is to have the clients believe in the new conception, and a persuasive argument must be thought out to accomplish that end.

≡ Relabeling Symptoms

Relabeling and reframing are components of the same procedure, because one often leads to the other; within the context of reframing, symptoms are frequently relabeled. By relabeling, however, a specific behavior or client characteristic is given a new name, the purpose being to aid the clients in reframing on their own.

Most often, therapists relabel individual behavior. Crying might be called expressing emotion, or controlling relabeled as structuring. On a system level, individual alcoholism is frequently relabeled as a family illness, or a family entering therapy is told that only a strong family could ask for help.

Whether relabeling at the individual or system levels, the new name can reflect either a change from positive to negative or vice versa. Examples of positive relabels that change a negative symbol to one less negative, or to neutral or positive include:

Temper tantrum: acting out, anger, expressing strong emotion

Beating child: spanking, swatting, disciplining

Withdrawal: silent, thoughtful

Drinking: medicating, anesthetizing

When clients minimize problems through labeling, a negative relabel might be called for. Negative relabeling consists of changing a positive label to one less socially desirable. Examples include the opposite of the positive relabels mentioned before and the following relabels:

Learning disabled: retarded

Extramarital fling: affair, intercourse

Close: strangling, smothering

As in reframing, the likelihood that a relabel will be adopted is primarily dependent on the esteem the client or the family holds for the therapist. If therapist esteem produced by reputation or client experience is high, clients are more likely to use the new label and attempt to change their actions. Where esteem for the therapist is low, relabeling will not be effective.

Instituting a change in labels can be conducted by merely using the new symbol when appropriate or by overtly discussing the label used by clients, asking them to use a different one, and explaining why. If the label that needs changing serves to control a wide range of family behavior, discussing the need for a different label is appropriate. For example, if a teenager is labeled a bad kid, the presenting problem includes violence, and the parents are considering foster care, a relabel of *strong-willed* or *immature* may change how the parents react and, accordingly, the child's behavior. Producing such major changes will be enhanced by openly discussing use of the label *bad kid* and the ramifications of creating more of a problem by continuing to use the label. Part of the discussion might include describing how the new label can be used in everyday family interaction and establishing clear guidelines of the new parenting behavior that will fit with the new label.

≡ Rewarding Clients

Therapists correctly assume that they are psychologically important to their clients, and that their approval can help clients change. The ways of showing that approval range from making a long statement that might follow successful completion of homework to simply stating, "Good." The longer statement has the most effect if it is stated in terms of the therapist's feelings. For example, if a father and son have successfully negotiated a rule on their own, their therapist might say, "I'm glad you two were able to sit down and calmly agree about the time you are to be in on school nights. Getting that issue settled has made me confident you can tackle your larger issues just as effectively."

Shorter rewarding remarks typically are used in situations when skills are being taught in session. When, a spouse responds as taught during a session in which a couple is being taught problem solving, for instance, a quick, unobtrusively stated "Good" or "That's it" immediately after an effective response will communicate approval. In teaching situations, such remarks need to occur frequently (approximately one per minute) until the client knows what is expected. Then the rate can be gradually lessened, but not eliminated. Appropriate behavior, if it is to continue and generalize, requires attention supplied through social reinforcement.

≡ Setting Up a Role Play

Whether for educational or therapeutic reasons, role play is used quite extensively by family therapists. In the initial phase of therapy, therapists often use role play to communicate family system concepts and to reframe symptoms. In the middle phase, role play can help clients experience contrasts between old and new behavior and the outcomes of each. Together with family sculpting and many psychodramatic techniques that are forms of role play, asking family members to take on roles and act them out in accordance with specific guidelines is a powerful procedure.

There are three rules to follow in setting up a role play. First, the doctrine of no surprises dictates that clients be forewarned that they may be expected to role-play. That means that if a therapist plans to conduct role play on some issue in a session, the clients should be told at the beginning of the session that they may be asked to role-play later on. Second, when it comes time to set up the role play, clients are not asked whether they would like to participate. Instead, the therapist moves participants into their roles without asking for cooperation. Third, and most important, the role-players need specific instructions regarding the setting and what they are to do.

In specifying the roles that players are to assume, detail is crucial. For example, if a husband and wife are to play out their last fight in order to discover how to avoid such flare-ups in the future, several pieces of information are required. The therapist should find out where the fight happened, how the spouses were feeling and what they were doing before the fight occurred, who said and did what during the fight, and how they ended it. Once these details are known, the couple will be able to act out the fight, because they will have refreshed their memories as to what happened.

Similarly, if clients are asked to engage in new behavior, detailed role descriptions will allow them to pay more attention to the role and less to figuring out what to do in that role. The easiest way to quickly provide the required amount of detail is for the therapist to model. When teaching time-out, for example, the role of the child and the role of the parent should be modeled first by the therapist, then tried on by the clients. As with all therapeutic procedures, many outcomes are possible when clients role-play. The likelihood that the outcome of a role play will be the one desired is enhanced by taking the time to set it up carefully.

Examples of what families can role-play are numerous. Couples can act out their latest scrap or how they compliment one another, providing greater understanding of what the spouses actually do to and with one another. In a family context, children and their parents can role-play stressful interactions to achieve the same end of providing added insight into interactional patterns and the possibilities for change. Finally, role play can be an extremely powerful educational tool. For example, instead of merely describing how parents are to use time-out with their children, a role-played situation in the therapy session in which a child pretends to misbehave and a parent implements time-out is an excellent opportunity for the therapist to observe and supervise parenting behavior.

≡ Client Out-of-Session Work

An interesting issue related to therapy homework and assignments is what to call out-of-session work by clients, and what labels to use in describing such activities during therapy sessions. Among some clients, because of their miserable school experience, the mere mention of the words *homework* or *assignment* will prompt an immediate and negative reaction if that is what out-of-session work is called. Other clients ascribe a positive connotation to the same labels, because their school careers were more satisfying. In either case, by determining clients' school experience in the assessment phase of theapy, an appropriate label can be used. Possibly the best tactic, however, is not to use any label at all.

Assigning Homework

There are several important factors that need to be kept in mind when considering what out-of-session work clients might do. The first is whether the clients are capable of carrying out the task. Nothing is gained, and perhaps much is lost, if spouses who cannot control their hostility in session are asked to go out on a date, for example, to refresh the romantic flavor of their relationship. Failure in this instance is likely, because if they could control their hostility, they would. The same reasoning applies to spouses who cannot share feelings with one another in session and are then asked to spend an hour at home discussing their feelings. If they knew how to do so, they would probably not be in therapy. Before couples like those just described are directed to perform such tasks, they need to have their emotional baggage cleared away, and they need to learn how to conduct themselves. Unless symptom exaggeration is the focus of therapy, clients benefit the most from out-of-session tasks that allow them to be successful, and to be successful, they must have the requisite skills before undertaking the task.

A second factor involves explaining why out-of-session work is important and what the potential gains from a task might be. As with other procedures, clients are cooperative if they know why they are asked to perform some task. Likewise, homework needs a rationale. Many therapists, however, do not take time to carefully explain how the homework fits into an overall treatment plan, nor do they specify the goals of the task. One or two sentences about the rationale and the goals usually does not suffice. Rather, a clear and persuasive statement is needed.

A third factor is the degree of specificity needed. To reduce the chance of misunderstanding and resistance, clients should know exactly what they are to do. In assigning spouses to talk with one another about some aspect of their relationship, compliance will be more likely if the time and place for the talk is scheduled when the assignment is made. Explanations can get too detailed, of course, but in general, the fewer decisions clients are forced to make about an assignment, the more likely they are to complete it successfully.

Homework Processing

In-session processing of homework is one of the most important aspects of therapy. As stated earlier, the goal of homework is to extend the influence of the therapist and the session into the everyday life of a family. Through post-session assignments, the therapist can enhance control over the awareness of family members and influence the family system toward some intended change. By asking clients about their assignment, the therapist accomplishes several important objectives.

First, but not foremost, asking about out-of-session work is an easy way to begin a session. After a while, the usual opening remark, "Well, [popularized by Ronald Reagan] . . ." gets very tiresome. A much more concrete executive remark is, "What happened this week with my recommendation that you spend less time talking about Sue's depression?" Notice that the assignment is restated, implying that the therapist recalls what occurred in the previous session. Post-session notes should always include assignments given to clients so that even with a very heavy caseload, a therapist can communicate more personal interest in clients' progress.

A second reason to ask about homework or assignments at the beginning of a session is to emphasize the importance of out-of-session work by making it the first order of business. In addition, dealing with assignments first ensures that they will not be forgotten. When a therapist assigns a task and then does not ask about it later on, the client can assume that the assignment was not important, and that perhaps other things the therapist says are not important. Spending session time on assignments is a way therapists can establish and maintain credibility.

A third reason is that since assignments often comprise the end of therapy sessions, beginning sessions with a report of the results of out-of-session work provides continuity between sessions and frames each session with related activities. Therapy sessions, like television programs or novels, need beginnings and endings. Although too much of a routine becomes boring, enough of one is needed for the therapist and clients to designate therapy as an event separate from other life activities; thus, the importance of framing sessions. Along with effective transitions from session to session comes a sense of direction and accomplishment especially needed in therapy.

The actual processing of homework can take several forms. When a therapist has clearly defined objectives for a particular session (for example, conduct a genogram) a short report by the clients may be all that is necessary. When a session is based on the outcome of an assignment which is the focus of therapy (such as a no-drinking contract, symptom-exaggerated), a more extended procedure is in order. Under these circumstances, the therapist will want to know what happened, how family members felt, and what they thought.

The first task in in-depth processing is to get a general overview of what happened. To obtain this information, the clients can be directed to give an overview without specifics. Once the therapist understands what happened in general, specific questions can be asked. In addition to supplying understanding, the questions should help to determine why the assignment was successful, that is, why it failed or met its goals. Clients' replies to the specific questions will create the content for the remainder of the session.

Clients Neglect or Change Out-of-Session Work

When clients either change or fail to complete out-of-session work, it is usually the fault of the therapist. Too often, assignments are not adequately explained or too many tasks are assigned. Also, clients are often asked to complete tasks they cannot perform. For example, asking spouses who have never been verbally intimate to talk for ten minutes, three times in the next week, is sure to fail. The results may be anything from a no-show at the next session to three bitter arguments. Similarly, asking parents to be more consistent in keeping family rules for teenagers, when no rules existed before, is also sure to result in more problems. If clients understand exactly what to do, and if they know how to do it, they will usually comply.

When the assignment is understood and clients have the skills to carry it out, but do not, or they change it, two interpretations are possible. One is that the relationship system may have been misread by the therapist, and the clients' fear of changing homeostasis may have prevented completing the task. Such "resistance" means the treatment plan may need reformulation. Perhaps the threat of change is too evident, and the pace of therapy needs slowing. It is more likely, however, that no real treatment plan existed, and the task was assigned out of habit or because it was the only task thought of on the spur of the moment. When a treatment plan has been constructed, and multiple instances of changed or incomplete homework occur, a switch out of structural to paradoxical methods may be required.

More typically, however, clients who possess the skills to complete homework tasks and fail, do not understand why they are to do the homework. Asking a couple or family to spend more time together, go out on a date, discuss a family rule, or whatever means they must be persuaded that completing the task is important and that it is a relevant part of the treatment process. By implication then, each homework assignment should be prefaced with a persuasive statement that specifies why the task is being assigned. Also, therapists with heavy caseloads must develop a system that prevents them from forgetting what was assigned or neglecting to process the assignment in the following session. The importance of homework assignments is supported by persuading clients to do them and following up on them in the next session with time devoted to discussing the outcome.

≡ Interrupting a Session to Change Interaction Patterns

Frequently, in the midst of a session, a therapist will observe a piece of interaction between clients that plays a role in maintaining either the symptom or a dysfunctional family structure. The dilemma is whether to interrupt the session and change the interaction or let it go, hoping it will occur again at a more opportune time. Experience will be the best guide on whether to intervene. Generally, however, it is best to intervene rather than wait until later; a better opportunity may not present itself.

Therapist willingness to interrupt a session primarily depends on the ability to smoothly stop interaction, transit to the intervention, make the intervention, then return to the original topic. For example, suppose a husband and wife are discussing their feelings of being trapped in their marriage. The wife states, "When I go out, you always quiz me about what I've been doing, who I was with, and where we went. Well, I . . ."

Therapist: "I'd like to interrupt here for a second. I need to comment on how you are talking together. Jane, I noticed that one of the words you used may stop your message from getting across. As much as possible, I would like both of you to try not using the words *always* or *never*. They tend to create an argument about how often something happens, then the real issue gets sidetracked. Now, say the same thing but leave out the argument word."

Wife: "When I go out, I don't like it when you ask me a lot of questions about who I was with, what we did, or where we went."

Therapist: "Good, go on."

Interrupting clients to make a change in their behavior is less threatening for the therapist who knows that it is possible to do so gracefully. Such interruptions end with the therapist's directing the clients to continue with what was interrupted.

≡ Reducing Family Loyalty

The book *Invisible Loyalties* (Boszormenyi-Nagy and Spark, 1973) loudly proclaimed the important role that family loyalties play in family processes. The authors skillfully portrayed the role of relationship ledgers and the importance that the balancing of these ledgers has in relationships. As a result, many family therapists initiated efforts to understand families in relation to loyalties. The two family life-cycle stages in which loyalties are most influential are as follows: the family with an adolescent and the newly married couple.

The family with an adolescent is typically confronted most dramatically with a member beginning to shift attention and allegiances outside of the family. Although this is not a problem for some families, others experience this shifting of loyalty as a form of rejection and heresy by the adolescent. This perception typically results in the family's becoming more constrictive and attempting to further prevent the adolescent from engaging in the age-appropriate process of beginning to leave home. Predictably, the adolescent responds by behaving in ways that are perceived as being even more dramatic evidence of wanting to leave, and the "runaway equation" effect develops in which the more the parents do something to squelch behavior, the more the adolescent feels that the only option is to escalate the behavior. This problem is particularly evident in families best described as enmeshed (Minuchin, 1974). Interestingly, these families are frequently those in which the parents themselves are still struggling with attempting to resolve loyalty issues with their families of origin.

This type of family is often helped by having the problem with the adolescent framed in the context of loyalty issues for the adolescent and that client's apprehensiveness about beginning to leave home. Helping the parents recall their own leaving-home process and then encouraging them to coach their youngster about leaving home can be very helpful. While the adolescent is getting what is wanted (leaving home and individuating), the parents gain some sense of control and involvement that eases their distress over feeling abandoned or rejected by the adolescent. During this time, it is important for the therapist to frame this process or place it in the context of a developmental process that is normal for our society. To describe the parents' facilitation of this process as a gift to the child can be helpful, as can identifying how the parents as a couple can be helpful to each other during this time. This suggestion serves to stabilize and strengthen the marital relationship that may otherwise seem jeopardized by the potential loss of an important family member. This crisis situation may be the first time the parents have ever openly discussed the issue of loyalty or commitment to the family. The act of openly discussing it may dislodge them from the unspoken fear and apprehension that has been blocking their engagement in the natural process of evolution from one stage of the family life cycle to the next.

The newly married couple is the other stage of family development during which the problem of family loyalties is most often observed. As the new spouses develop and organize their own relationship, attempting to incorporate rules and patterns from their respective families of origin, loyalty problems may surface. These issues can arise because one of the spouses feels disloyal to his or her own family and must fight to have old family patterns incorporated into this new family, or the spouse may be stimulated by one or more parents who feel abandoned. This apparent crisis can often be used to motivate the young couple to make a commitment to focus on the type of family the couple wants to develop; specifically, what the couple most wants to bring into this new family from the families of origin, and what the couple most wants to leave behind.

The process of having the spouses talk concretely and specifically about these issues takes the loyalty struggle out of the shadows of their current relationship, and places it clearly in perspective. This intervention places the process of the couple's developing a new relationship in a new context; it becomes purposeful and future-oriented rather than one contaminated by the past and by the pull of being loyal to the spouses' respective families. Therapy consists of developing a loyalty to the couple's own relationship, and a negotiation process to aid the transition.

≡ Changing the Seating Pattern

As has been noted by many therapists, the seating pattern chosen by clients often indicates family structure. After the initial phase of therapy, seating patterns may change from one session to the next to reflect new coalitions or alliance breakups. As part of treatment, a therapist may choose to change a seating pattern to symbolize new family structure or to make an intervention easier.

Changing a seating pattern is an easy task that can be made difficult, if not impossible. If a therapist pleads for the clients' permission, the likelihood of noncompliance increases. The change is easy if the therapist says, "George, I'd like you to change seats with Marjorie. That will make it easier for you two to talk directly to one another." Typically, clients will cooperate. If George balks, the therapist can stand up, grasp him gently by the arm, gesture him to stand, and steer him over to Marjorie's seat. If she does not move, the therapist can use the same physical management to get her to stand and move to George's seat. The easiest way to get clients to cooperate in changing seats is to direct them to do so without requesting permission or creating the opportunity for a battle for structure.

FACILITATING MORE EFFECTIVE PARENTING

≡ Enhancing the Parental Alliance

As part of the assessment process, the state or condition of the parental subsystem can be indexed to analyze this aspect of family health. A breach

in the parental alliance is easily detected from observations of family interaction or reports from family members. For instance, the children state that
mom and dad have different rules; the parents complain that one is more
lenient than the other; or one parent is responsible for all child care, leaving
the other with no real parenting role. What can be done to strengthen the
parental subsystem?

At the root of a broken or weak parental alliance is a lack of agreement
on parenting standards and a lack of joint decision making on a day-to-day
basis. The first step in changing these weaknesses involves requiring the
parents to carry out their role during sessions. At all times, parents should be
maintained in their role. When mild disagreements between parents occur
in-and out-of-session, discussions of parenting standards can be undertaken.
The objective of these discussions is to arrive at agreement on standards.

More effective, however, is joint decision making that takes place as
incidents occur that require parenting. For example, when children become
noisy and distracting in session, the parents can be prompted to intervene.
When they handle a situation poorly, the therapist can model what has been
labeled the bathroom procedure (Smets, 1985). Several steps are involved.
First, the parents and the therapist leave the consulting room and meet in a
nearby bathroom to discuss how the parents are going to handle the children. The therapist helps them decide on a course of action that they are to
carry out in the session. Upon returning to the session, the children are asked
to act up again, and the parents act on their agreement. The homework
assignment consists of bathroom meetings at home whenever the children
require guidance. The bathroom procedure requires that both parents get
involved, and it helps focus parental attention on bigger child management
problems while decreasing attention to minor events.

☰ Describing the Parent Role

One reason that parents abuse or neglect their children lies in their
misconception of the parent role. Helping children and their parents in such
instances involves more than teaching child guidance and parent-child
relationship skills. It is often instructive for the therapist to define effective
parenting at an intellectual level, and in so doing change parents' expectations of themselves. The following is an example:

I'd like to spend a few minutes defining the role of an effective
parent. Raising children is a very difficult job. It takes a lot of time and a
lot of hard work. By their nature, children need to be taught how to do
nearly everything, and one part of being a parent is teaching them what
they need to know. What that boils down to is being patient and
understanding. When a child misbehaves, they may be seeking atten-

tion, or more frequently, they simply don't know how to do anything other than misbehave. Changing how your kids act is a long and frustrating job; no parent has a child who learns after being told how to behave just once. Part of parenting is telling children how to act over and over again.

Another aspect of parenting includes punishing children. Research has pretty well shown that hitting children has side effects that in the long run produce more problems. Put a lot of effort into trying not to hit your kids. Use time-out or loss of TV, allowance, or dinner as punishment.

Children also need to spend time with you. It is not enough to park them in front of the TV for most of their waking hours. If taught, even the smallest child can do some part of the work needed to keep a household running. Working together is equivalent to any other activity performed together except, perhaps, just listening to children talk about their day or their troubles.

Like it or not, the parent role means more giving than receiving. Children do give back, but not in equal measure for the time and energy they take. Your parents may not have understood that, but it is up to you to change the style of parenting that has been present in your families perhaps for generations.

≡ Parents Will Not Control Children in Session

The opportunity to observe how parents interact with their children can prove invaluable to the therapist. As with most interactional behavior, though, eventually patterns already observed repeat themselves, and little, if any, new behavior is observed. This is one reason there is no sense in allowing disruptive and disturbing children to continue to act out during sessions. Another reason may be concern for the safety of the therapist's office and belongings and the personal safety of all. Further, assuming the parents are unable to productively control their children, not to do anything about the kids may simply add to the parents' sense of embarrassment and futility, and lead them to prematurely terminate therapy. For these reasons, it is important for the therapist to promote some new behaviors among parents with disruptive children.

One procedure to implement with disruptive children is to encourage the parents to intervene with them. This gives the therapist the chance to observe parenting styles and offer feedback on how the parents might improve or add to their management style and repertoire. Many times, parents are quite unaware of the variety of management strategies available, and they continue to relate to their children with an impoverished parental arsenal. In these cases, providing information can be tremendously helpful. For instance, teaching parents techniques such as time-out or the Premack principle of exchanging high-probability behavior for low-probability behavior can be energizing. Perhaps the parents threaten the children with consequences they are highly unlikely to enforce. Such parents can benefit from learning how they create ongoing struggles for themselves. Regardless, it is important for the therapist to begin to intervene and model a sense of competency for the parents. Along with information, the therapist can also help the parents by encouraging them and providing them with support and reinforcement for their accomplishments.

At other times, the therapist may choose to model implementing child management techniques with the children. For instance, the therapist may use time-out with a child during the course of a session, or utilize the Pemack principle by informing the child that if she sits in a particular fashion for a designated length of time, she can then play with a particular toy for a few minutes. The therapist may also simply model the direct and clear communication of expectations to a child, unlike the equivocal and apologetic style typically employed by the parents. This modeling can be followed up by coaching the parents on how they might do the same, fully expecting children to test whether or not this new behavior of the parents is for real.

There are also times when children are disturbing to the therapist but not to parents. In these instances, a therapist should act anyway and not allow the children to violate their standards. This is particularly true when a therapist feels that their ability to attend to the family is impaired by child disruptiveness or are concerned about the safety of personal belongings in their office. Although the therapist may want to consider child-proofing the office, it is unreasonable to do this and then end up with unspoken resentments toward a family. In these cases, therapists should clearly identify their needs and expectations, avoiding, as much as possible, demeaning or condemning behavior. For instance, a possible request might be worded as follows: "Would you please have the children stop that? Perhaps I'm overly sensitive, but I find it very difficult to listen to you the way I want to with that happening," or "Would you keep the kids from doing that, please? Those [some personal belongings in the office] are very valuable to me and I don't want anything to happen to them." In all likelihood, if therapists model this type of self-affirmation and directness, it will prove helpful to most families, regardless of the presenting problem.

≡ Interacting with Young Children

The family therapy process usually includes young children. A prominent danger in working with their families is to ignore the young children, only addressing the adults and older children who are capable of speaking the same logical language that the therapist does. In doing so, therapists deny themselves the rich advantage of joining the family through young children and the benefit of the understanding so often afforded by the young, who can utter truths without defensiveness characteristic of adults and teenagers.

Few parents can avoid developing feelings of fondness for those who positively attend to their young children. Consequently, therapists who are kind, attentive, and interactive with a family's young children are bound to engender fondness in the parents toward them. To avoid this simple, but powerful, means of initially joining the family is a gross oversight. Attending to children also conveys to the family that children are valued in the therapy context, and they are perceived as being as much a part of the family as any other member. Further, such attention can serve to model, for one or both parents, how to effectively interact with young children. Typically, it will be a more valuable lesson for the father than the mother.

Interacting with the children can also quickly provide valuable information about the structure and operation of the family. For instance, interacting in the following fashion with the four-year-old who clutches his teddy bear closely to his chest upon entering the room, can produce valuable insights:

> That teddy bear looks as though he gives you lots of good feelings. I had one like that when I was your age and I loved him as much as it looks like you love that one. It's nice to feel close, isn't it? Who else in this family can you cuddle with like you can cuddle with your teddy? How about your brother over there; who can he cuddle with? How about Dad, Mom, etc.?

Using the child's world, and whatever toy might be important to the child, can provide a valuable path to a quick understanding of important dimensions of the family's structure and operating schema. A child's responses can disclose where the alliances and coalitions are, who the child looks to for permission to speak, what silencing mechanisms are employed by the family to keep children quiet, which family member is overresponsible for the children and tries to get them to say the right thing, and other equally important bits of information relevant to the development of a therapeutic plan.

As suggested by Haley (1976), it is always valuable to have toys and puppets available in the therapy room, to give children the opportunity to communicate in play form. Toys not only provide a conduit for the children to convey their messages, but also provide a means of assessing how the parents play with the children and what skills parents have for interacting with their children in the child's world. Having toys available provides the opportunity to tap into children's intuitive world, which tends to be more sensitive to emotion than adult cognitive powers. Drawing paper, crayons, chalkboard, chalk, finger paints, blocks, dolls, and a dollhouse all provide a communication channel for children. Toys also provide children with the opportunity to escape into fantasy when the therapy process proves too much for their developing egos.

Having children present in the sessions also provides the therapist the opportunity to directly observe the parent-child interaction style prevalent in the family. Once the style has been observed, specific interventions to assist in the development of more positive parenting techniques can be offered. In addition, having children present, and interacting with them, promotes the preventive component of family therapy. Children have the opportunity to participate firsthand in the process of effecting family change, acquiring this learning which they can use to prevent similar problems in their future relationship spheres.

ATTENDANCE AT SESSIONS

≡ Client Shows Up without Partner

When one partner comes to a session without the other, a choice is presented to the therapist: whether to go ahead with the session with one partner, or wait until the next time both can attend. Generally speaking, if a therapeutic alliance is established with the couple, an individual session can occur without damage, assuming certain precautions are taken. On the other hand, if it is doubtful that the alliance has been established with the couple, an individual session could prove difficult to the development of future couple-oriented work.

Assuming the couple appears to be engaged sufficiently, an individual session could be productive in addressing items such as family-of-origin issues for the partner present. This is particularly true when a client's history includes issues such as an alcoholic parent or physical or sexual abuse. The couple alliance can be protected by suggesting that the session with the spouse be tape-recorded, so that the absent spouse can listen to it prior to the next conjoint session, or by having the understanding that this session will be reviewed with the absent spouse at the next session. It is also valuable to relate to the spouse seen individually that the therapist preserves the prerogative of determining what needs to be shared with the absent spouse. Establishing this rule prior to beginning the session can serve to prevent the attending spouse from being tempted to develop an unfair alliance with the therapist by sharing a secret. If this rule is not clearly stated, a secret can put the therapist in a compromised position, with the spouse present thinking they have a different and special relationship. This can prove counterproductive to the future conjoint therapy. Surprisingly, stating this rule to the spouse present can also be reassuring, because of the realization that this is a therapist who will neither allow nor promote the debilitating effect of secrets.

If therapy has just been initiated, the therapist may tell the spouse present that an individual session at this stage of therapy may prove destructive, and reschedule another conjoint session. Typically, a statement by the therapist such as the following proves sufficient:

> It is my experience that to conduct an individual session at this stage of therapy proves counterproductive, and out of fairness to the two of you I believe it is important for us to reschedule another appointment when both can be present. I realize this may not make sense to you at this time, but hopefully, you can trust me that I want to be of the most help possible, and this is the best way.

Naturally, this is a situation that can usually be avoided by clearly stating during the initial session that both partners, or all the family members, need to be present for any session to be conducted, unless the therapist indicates otherwise in advance.

The process of rescheduling another session may be irritating to the spouse present, but simultaneously, it will likely convey that the therapist is a professional who is consistent and strong. If a client has come from a chaotic and underorganized family of origin, the therapist's decision to reschedule can develop the client's sense of confidence, and it also allows the therapist to model how to say what he or she means and then following through. In this respect, the struggle for determining the structure of the therapy, which the therapist should determine, is maintained, and it better ensures that the initiative or work to be done will be up to the clients.

The precautions that apply to a one-partner session also apply to therapy work with entire families. If the therapist has requested the entire family show up for a session, but one or more members are absent, the therapist is confronted by the same dilemma. To proceed without these members present may communicate that although the therapist values the entire family, the therapist's behavior communicates otherwise. Obviously, this message can be a dangerous one for the family to believe, as they begin to wonder about what else the therapist said but did not really mean.

≡ Client Asks for Individual Session

When one family member requests an individual session, the therapist needs to address that person's intentions, as well as the perceptions of the others. Even if it does not seem that there is anything that needs to be said in an individual session that could not be said in the couple/family context, it is important to adequately process these requests. If the request comes in the context of a couple/family session, the therapist can clarify the intent of the person making it and the perceptions and concerns of the others present. If the request seems appropriate and the others do not react adversely, the session can be conducted, but with the therapist's conditions identified ahead of time. Some valuable conditions that might be communicated include the following: the therapist has the prerogative of choosing what to bring into the couple/family work from the individual session; the session will be audiotaped so that others not present can review it before the next conjoint session; the person attending the individual session must assume responsibility for sharing the outcome with the others; and the therapist will clarify the focus and intent of the individual session with all members present, with no digressions from this focus allowed.

In the case of a family member who disagrees with another member's desire for an individual session, the disagreement should be resolved between the clients, not by the therapist. The processing of this disagreement, and the apparent suspicion it reveals, can prove valuable to understanding the organization and operation of the clients' relationship. Frequently, this disagreement reflects other tensions and differences present in the relationship.

There may be times when the therapist believes individual sessions are indicated. For instance, assume a couple has been seen for several sessions and a sound therapeutic alliance is present. The couple informs the therapist that one of them will be out of town, or otherwise occupied, at the time of the next scheduled session, and the therapist determines it would be an appropriate time to address such issues as family-of-origin concerns with the one client available. Discussing the intent of the individual session and determining the reactions of each spouse prior to scheduling will usually avoid provoking suspiciousness or distance and can be used to continue to provoke positive change instead.

Choosing to amplify an alliance with a particular family member is another example of a time calling for an individual session. One instance might be when spouses present themselves for conjoint work out of primary concern for the husband's drinking. Assume the wife presents herself as angry, at wit's end, and obviously committed to therapy, while her husband is just as obviously exercising caution, concerned that the therapist will just be an extension of his wife who, according to his perception, has a combative nature. Considering that the wife appears invested in therapy, she will likely accept an individual session between the therapist and husband without feeling unduly threatened. After all, the husband is in therapy and this is what she has wanted for some time. The individual session can be used to relate to the husband in a nonaccusatory fashion, and to develop his sense of trust and belief in the therapist's competency and desire to provoke positive change, rather than a belief that the therapist is someone who needs to be defended against. In this regard, the individual session facilitates the conjoint work and, perhaps in this case, increases the ease of confronting the issue of the alcohol problem without activating too much resistance.

≡ Clients Do Not Show for Session

Most clinics and practitioners today have a rule specifying a cost for any session that the clients miss without giving prior notification. This rule is important to enforce, because it communicates to clients that the therapist's time is valuable, and models self-valuation to them. At times, at least a portion of the family problem is poor organization and low capacity for following through on decisions. Allowing families to be irresponsible about the time committed to them by the therapist cannot be condoned. Although all of us experience the unexpected, and even emergencies, at times, promoting irresponsibility on the part of clients is not productive. Perhaps the first missed appointment can be excused because of an emergency that arose, but to do so consistently is to invite more such incidents.

A call after the first missed appointment can serve to convey the therapist's concern about the clients' behavior. On very rare occasions, a second missed appointment might call for another direct statement of the therapist's concern about the family's interest and commitment to the therapeutic process. This phone call might sound something like this:

> I'm calling about the appointment that was missed today. I realize there could be many reasons, but hopefully you can appreciate that my time is valuable and that I cannot afford these missed times. As explained to you in our first meeting, I will charge for missed appointments. I'm wondering what might be done to avoid this happening again in the future; would another scheduled time within my regular hours perhaps be helpful, or what ideas might you have?

At other times it may be more convenient for the therapist to send a letter instead, and in fact, many therapists have a form letter to send at these times. The letter would have essentially the same content as the sample phone conversation, and depending upon circumstances, convey to the family that the therapist will assume therapy is terminated unless informed differently by a specified deadline (within two weeks, for example).

Keeping in mind the fact that many families seen in clinical settings are underorganized, it is important that the therapist seize the missed appointment as an opportunity to communicate to the family the importance of structure/organization, that the therapist values self enough to adhere to established rules, and that behavior has consequences. As mentioned, although there are always exceptions to rules, the behavior of missing appointments must generally have certain consequences attached to it, or else the therapist may fall into the trap of unwittingly encouraging more irresponsible and underorganized behavior by the family.

☰ Engaging an Unwilling Family Member

Throughout the family therapy literature, the firm sense is that therapy with entire families is the treatment of choice. Consequently, therapists should not be afraid to refuse service to a part of a family or to postpone an interview appointment to a time all family members can be present. An alternative to refusing service, however, is to actively attempt to influence uncooperative family members.

In most cases, the IP's spouse or other family members will come in for at least one session. Positive reframing and extensive joining might seduce the visitor into becoming a full-time participant. Typically, unavailable partners or unwilling family members will attend sessions if personally requested to by the therapist. Reframing their presence with the idea "Help me help your family" can be a useful tactic. Stanton, Todd, and Associates (1982) suggest that several home visits by the therapist may increase family member cooperation.

Another approach is to start therapy with one spouse or a partial group, but concentrate discussions on how to get the missing client(s) into therapy. The therapist should keep in mind that there may be powerful resistance on the part of all involved members to the participation of other family members. Many times, however, cooperating clients do not know how to phrase a request for their partner's participation or fear their ability to explain therapy to a child. In-session practice of how to explain therapy and the need to have the partner's cooperation in attending sessions are appropriate in these instances.

When these more straightforward approaches do not elicit participation, other strategies can be used. The therapist might call an unwilling spouse during a session with the other spouse and state, "I'm Dr. So-and-So and your wife [husband] is here in therapy. I'm hearing her [his] side of the story and I would like to hear yours. Can you join us next week?" If the answer is, "No," the response might be: "You mean you'll leave changing the relationship up to her [him]? Well, I'll try to protect your interests, but I can't promise you all that much," or "As your wife [husband] changes, you may find yourself being depressed without knowing why." Along these same lines, the cooperating spouse can be coached to tease an unwilling partner by making comments at home that catch the interest of the unwilling partner such as, "The therapist thought you'd feel that way," or "The therapist thinks I have too much of the power in our marriage," or "The therapist said that adolescents need to have more of a chance to make decisions on their own than we have been allowing you."

The most common result of the clinician's use of these procedures is whole family participation in therapy. The pragmatics of professional practice dictate, however, that family therapists broaden their theory and skill base to include methods of working with individuals that produce whole-family changes.

≡ Geographically Unavailable Clients

As society has become more mobile, the problem of absent family members has been encountered more frequently. From a family systems perspective, helping parts of families may end up being problematic, may take place at the expense of those not present, and may lead to long-range problems. For instance, imagine a family that is in treatment as a result of the father's alcoholism, and the therapist leaves out an adult child because of geographic unavailability. The absent member may become the family scapegoat and be assigned a troublesome role in the family that serves only to reproduce the family's basic structure with a different person occupying a certain role. Whereas the family used to be occupied with father's dysfunction, now they have changed to being consumed with the problem of the member absent from therapy.

Because of these concerns, it is important to ensure the involvement of all in the therapeutic process. Although great distances and responsibilities may exist that interfere with all being present for therapy (such as the family in therapy in Nebraska with one member going to college on the East Coast) they may be accommodated. For instance, each session can have an empty chair present to represent the absent member, with a tape recorder placed on it. At the end of each session, the family mails that audiotape to the absent member, with the understanding that the absent member will respond to the tape with a tape recording, phone call, or letter. The increasing availability of portable video cameras presents an option that is even richer than the audiotape. Another, though more expensive, option is to use a speaker phone that allows a group to converse with a person on the other end of the line. This innovation presents an opportunity for immediate interaction not provided by making tapes but is more expensive. Many families have resolved this problem by sharing the expense among themselves, recognizing that all may reap the benefits. In the absence of these options, or in conjunction with them, letter writing can keep the absent member informed, with the added value that the writing responsibility is shared among the members present.

Regardless of the method employed to involve unavailable members, the availability of resources today and the value of using them seem to leave no excuse for not following through with one. Even disregarding the efficacy of this approach, it would still seem that family therapists are professionally responsible for making these options and the importance of taking advantage of them known to families.

DIFFICULT CLINICAL SITUATIONS

☰ Negotiating a No-Drinking Contract

The use of alcohol and other drugs by family members can prove to be a major problem that needs to be addressed before other changes can be effected. When a spouse presents a significant concern for the other spouse's drinking, the negotiation of a contract can prove helpful. The contract can be developed into a quid pro quo, or behavioral exchange, in which the one spouse relinquishes drinking behavior in exchange for a particular behavior desired from the other. The very act of negotiating this type of exchange can benefit the couple by demonstrating a new process of securing change in the relationship, without one of them feeling as though he or she has lost.

This process can be facilitated by asking the couple to generate a list of what they would like more of, or less of, from the other. Upon exchanging and examining each other's lists, they are then asked to attach a weighted value, based on their perspectives, to each of the listed items. For example, as the wife examines the list of wants/desires identified by the husband, she places a numeral, from one to ten, next to each item. It is understood that the numeral one placed next to an item means that it would be easy for her to do, requiring little effort and without giving her a sense of compromising herself too much, while ten would reflect a major effort or sense of compromising herself. Once the spouses have identified their respective values for each item on the other's list, they can then negotiate trade-offs by exchanging the weighted behaviors. The trade-off may consist of packages in which, for example, the wife agrees to exchange two behaviors she weighted at three and four in exchange for a behavior her husband weighted with a value of seven. There are times, however, when the spouse's drinking seems to be out of control to such a degree that this type of exchange is not effective in producing change.

In such a case, the therapist may choose to develop a different type of contract, one which is referred to as the Acid Test or the Marty Mann Test. Marty Mann, a recovering alcoholic herself, founded the National Council on Alcoholism over forty-five years ago. This contract is based upon the notion that loss of control, or the inability to limit one's drinking to reasonable amounts that do not result in harmful consequences or negative circumstances, is a substantial sign of addictive drug use. To develop this contract, the person is asked to identify how many drinks per day they could have before problems occurred. Once a number has been identified, the person is asked to stay within this self-prescribed limit for a period of four to six weeks. To make the contractual period much shorter than this could diminish the hoped-for effect. The rationale for this contract period is that during a period of four to six weeks, most humans will experience significant stressors in their lives, such that if they are problem drinkers, their inability to control their intake will be evidenced. If the person proves unable to control intake during this period, the problem drinker is asked to engage in an assessment of the problem drinking behavior with a person certified to conduct the assessment. During the period of time that the contract is in effect, the other spouse is asked to leave the monitoring of the drinking to the therapist and to the drinking spouse. The hope is that the non-drinking spouse can resolve some of the anxiety attached to the other's drinking and begin to detach emotionally from it, avoiding behaviors that otherwise might provoke the drinking spouse and serve as an excuse to drink.

Some will say that this type of contract cannot work, because the drinking spouse could just become more secretive about drinking and lie. While this is certainly is true, the drinker will know whether or not he or she has been true to the contract, and this is another way of "spitting in the soup" of the drinker. The drinker can continue to eat his or her soup, but it probably will not be as tasty or gratifying as it was before. In this respect, the process is another way of making the drinking more costly or less satisfying to the problem drinker. Also, the non-drinking spouse may be overly reactive to the drinking behavior of the other spouse, as a result of having been raised in a home with an alcoholic parent and receiving physical or sexual abuse when that parent was intoxicated. Certainly, it is understandable, but the overly reactive spouse can probably benefit from realizing that although this reaction had survival value in his or her family of origin, this is a different relationship.

≡ Structuring a Therapeutic Separation

The objective of separation is change—change in the direction of greater closeness or distance. Hopefully, old interactional patterns can be interrupted through creation of an environment that is more favorable to positive and productive change.

Granvold and Tarrant (1983) offer the following factors which may provide the rationale for a couple to implement a therapeutic separation:

1. The conflict has become so intense in the relationship that the aversiveness present limits the potential for any positive change.

The therapist may have much more leverage for introducing change if the spouses have only brief contacts through the benefits of the structure provided by the negotiated elements of the separation.

2. The couple's relationship has a history of low reward-exchange (exchange of pleasures, satisfactions, and gratifications). A separation may increase the potential for raising the level of mutual positive exchange between spouses and for experiencing greater freedom from a marriage that has become unrewarding.

3. One or both partners have a sense of being restricted or bound by the other or by the relationship, and may benefit from a respite.

4. The problems of sexual unhappiness or involvement of a third party may benefit from a separation that promotes experimentation without complete dissolution of the marriage. As with the other factors listed above, experimentation would need to be negotiated and agreed upon by both partners if it were to be a part of the separation.

5. A situational or midlife crisis may enhance the value of a structured separation. Separation may be better than divorce, with its long-range consequences. During a transition point in a person's life, deciding to separate can introduce a greater potential for objective decision making.

6. The separation can help stop one or both spouses from taking the other for granted and introduce greater objectivity into their perception of the marriage.

7. The separation can approximate life after an actual divorce. In this respect, a couple can try the separation as a test of what divorce might be like for them and of their individual potential for developing greater independent living skills and emotional independence.

In creating the structure through which spouses might more genuinely make an autonomous move toward or away from their relationship, and in assessing their individual and relationship needs more objectively, all can benefit from addressing certain issues (Barnard and Corrales, 1979). The spouses should incorporate these issues into their separation agreement, although the therapist should feel free to suggest them for their consideration.

1. Address the length of the separation to be negotiated, recognizing that six to twelve weeks is most often identified as reasonable.

2. Divorce is not to be used as a threat during the separation, and it is usually best to agree not to consult attorneys during this time.

3. Frequency of contact and arrangements for dating each other should be addressed, if the spouses agree.

4. The issues of the children's residence and visitation should also be negotiated.

5. What to tell friends, children, and others about the separation can be discussed and agreed upon.
6. Involvement of the spouses with others, sexually or otherwise, during the separation should be addressed. Hopefully, the spouses will understand the potential destructive effect of becoming involved with others during the separation.
7. The nature of sexual contact between the two spouses during the separation is another important point to address.
8. The role and goal of therapy during the separation should be agreed upon. How often? Individual or conjoint? Goals to be addressed?

These are examples of the kinds of questions that will need to be negotiated for the separation.

It is true that a structured separation can be used for devious purposes by one or both of the spouses, but the family therapist needs to acknowledge that it is *their* separation. The therapist is merely a consultant to their negotiations, and hopefully, one who can share some insights derived from past experience with the process.

≡ Affair Disclosed to Therapist Alone

When a client discloses a secret affair, unknown to the other spouse, the therapist's access to this secret can prove very debilitating to the therapeutic process. The therapist who colludes with one spouse in maintaining this secret runs the risk of being effectively paralyzed in the context of conjoint therapy, and of promoting an artificial sense of specialness or grandiosity in the spouse colluded with. Either one of these developments can prove extremely counterproductive to therapy.

To prevent this from occurring, the therapist can clearly state to each of the spouses during intake,

> Out of fairness to each of you, and myself, I will not accept phone calls between sessions, or in any other way be party to keeping secrets. It is my experience that secrets shared with the therapist do not prove helpful to therapy, and my potential for being helpful to you in the future becomes seriously impaired, if not destroyed, by allowing secrets to be shared with me. You need to understand that whatever information I become aware of, I will determine when and how it will be shared among all of us. Without this understanding, and an agreement regarding this issue, there is little sense in our proceeding.

Should this agreement not be kept, and information about an affair is communicated to the therapist, it is important to address it directly and stand by the intent of policy set initially, even to the point of terminating therapy. To do otherwise puts the therapist in the position of being so compromised that effectiveness is, at best, questionable.

For this reason, it is important to state the rule at the outset of therapy, so all involved are forewarned of the consequences of attempting to share secrets with the therapist. Hopefully, then, the therapist will not end up in the position of being declared unfair, unethical, and so on when termination is suggested for violating the rule. If the therapist does not make this point clear at the outset, the therapist becomes vulnerable to receiving a phone call between sessions and having a secret revealed, and then having to deal with the issue after the fact, which is always more difficult.

≡ Client Expresses Sexual Attraction toward Therapist

Perhaps it is less common among family therapists, because we tend to work with more than one client in the consulting room, but inevitably, over the course of a psychotherapeutic career, several clients will reveal they are sexually attracted to their therapist. While perhaps flattering, such a revelation can create an unpleasant situation, unless it is handled well. If dealt with poorly, the client's self-esteem may be affected, therapy may become sidetracked, the client may terminate, or a malpractice suit may result.

Handling the revelation effectively consists of a multistep procedure. Listening and communicating understanding of the client's feelings make up the first step. Some clients reveal their attraction in a sincere attempt to further therapy, while others disclose their feelings to distract and de-skill their therapist. Listening serves to help the therapist control reactions and to understand the client's motivation. After listening, a statement of a therapist's professional responsibility regarding sexual involvement with clients is needed to clarify that no sexual interaction will occur even though the therapist is flattered to be considered attractive. To aid the client in regaining composure after what amounts to rejection, it is helpful to explain that the therapeutic relationship often produces such feelings. Finally, the client's attention should be directed either toward him- or herself or toward changing existing intimate relationships.

When a client repeatedly expresses attraction, he or she should be told that this behavior is equivalent to sexual harassment. In such instances, a colleague should be consulted for supervision and support.

≡ Presenting Problem: Deciding to Divorce or Stay Married

Couples remain stuck over the decision of whether to divorce or remain married, primarily because they do not have the information required to weigh one alternative over the other. Divorce and marriage seem equally onerous and equally attractive. Only with new information can spouses get off the fence, and it is the therapist's job to provide it. One procedure that helps illuminate the pros and cons of either course is termed *planning the divorce*. The objective of such planning is to stop thinking that has become nonproductive and to dump new information into the dyad. The procedure has several stages.

Even though spouses experience their relationship as being in jeopardy, the therapist must first reframe their hesitancy in making a decision. Words such as these are appropriate:

> Your decision to remain undecided is most definitely a stay-married decision because you are still married. A decision to get divorced is a difficult one that requires a good deal of information you do not currently have. In my experience, our best tack is to map out in detail how you would divorce, along with careful discussion of the possible ramifications and likely results. In no way am I suggesting that you should divorce, but I am asking you to stop being undecided for the moment, to thoroughly examine the alternative to staying married and thinking about divorce.

In the second step, the divorce process is described in detail so that both spouses understand the time lines and the legal procedures involved. An outline of the decisions required such as child custody, dividing assets, relations with in-laws, and the nature of the post-divorce relationship should be discussed. After outlining the decisions, each one should be negotiated with special emphasis on detailing the post-divorce relationship between the spouses. How often are they to be in contact? How can they keep in touch (letter or phone)? Do they want to be friends, acquaintances, lovers, enemies, or what? Is sex OK after divorce? Can they seek counsel from one another? Negotiating these decisions typically requires several sessions.

The simple result of planning the divorce is usually greater clarity about why divorce is an option rather than clarity about working for a more successful marriage. Also, once the partners have a clearer view of the gains and losses that might result from the divorce, motivation for working on the marriage tends to increase and treatment can proceed.

≡ One Spouse Secretly Wishes to Divorce

When one spouse appears to be dragging his or her feet and resisting the flow and direction of therapy, it is possible that a desire for divorce is being masked. In these cases, the spouse may be in therapy for any of these types of reasons: to appease others and to show an effort at "trying" before divorcing; to attempt to develop a relationship between the spouse and the therapist so the leaving can be easier, or to alleviate a sense of guilt or the fear of the other spouse possibly committing suicide at the time of divorce.

The therapist can confront the resistance and foot dragging directly and appropriately declare the impotence that is present, for example:

> In view of the number of assignments that have not been attempted, or only half-heartedly so, and the missed appointments and ongoing disagreements we have, I am confused about your reported desire to improve this marriage. While I am willing to assume some responsibility and believe that perhaps my notion of how to help does not fit with your notions, we appear to be stuck and not moving at all in the direction you reported wanting to move. I mentioned at the outset of this therapy that I could be of assistance in certain ways, but could not do the work for you. At this point, I believe either I cannot be of help to you because we do not fit, or I question the sincerity of your stated goal of wanting to improve the marriage, and wonder if you either want to continue the relationship as it has been, or perhaps you want out of it entirely. Is it possible you are not being entirely candid with either yourself or me in your stated intention?

After having made this declaration, it is important to process it and determine reactions. At these times, a therapist must attempt to monitor his or her own ego investment in the therapy, and avoid becoming stuck and subsequently defensive and/or attacking. Certainly, a defensive posture by the therapist will not prove facilitative to productive processing of this issue.

≡ New Information Revealed at the End of a Session

Occasionally, a member of a family will regularly express a desire to communicate "something very important" when there are only a few minutes left in the session. Although from time to time, as a natural evolution of a particular session, someone may disclose something that requires a few extra minutes beyond the scheduled time, some clients attempt to do so with regularity. With these clients, it is amazing how unusual it is for the important information to be important. Most typically, end-of-session disclosure is an effort to postpone the termination of the session, to test the therapist's capacity for maintaining some control of the session, a means of attracting extra attention, or some combination of these factors.

When this practice seems to be a pattern, rather than a chance occasion, it is important that the therapist not inadvertently reinforce this behavior. A valuable way to address this problem is to say: "From the urgency on your face [or "the way you are presenting this" or "from hearing what you've said so far"] it is apparent to me that this is too important to address in the few short minutes remaining. Out of fairness to you, I would far rather wait until our next session and address this at the outset, so we can give it proper attention." After having said this, it is important to bring the issue back to attention at the start of the next session. Interestingly, however, the issue frequently turns out to have been discussed or resolved and no longer possesses the same degree of urgency suggested at the last meeting.

If the behavior continues, despite the therapist's efforts (and this is, indeed, a rare occurrence), the therapy can probably benefit from the therapist's confronting the issue more directly, stating something like:

> If I recall correctly, this is about the fifth or sixth time you've brought up an issue that seems to have some degree of urgency attached to it at the end of a session. Because of the time crunch we are confronted with in the last few minutes of a session, it proves distressing to me, and I'm assuming it must be equally uncomfortable for you. What do you believe accounts for this, and what can be done to avoid either one of us having to be uncomfortable like this in the future?

In all likelihood, ignoring such behavior will only promote more of it in the future. This continuation will likely culminate in mutual dislike between therapist and client and, in any case, it is unlikely to be a positive influence on therapy.

≡ Addressing Violent Relationships

In her highly acclaimed book *The Battered Woman*, Walker (1979) identified three distinct phases in violent relationships. She describes phase one as consisting of minor incidents of violence, which gradually escalate in seriousness and finally culminate in a phase two, or acute battering, incident. Phase two is generally no longer in duration than twenty-four hours, and is followed by phase three, called the "honeymoon phase." This phase consists of a cessation of the violence and an expression of remorse on the part of the violent partner, who becomes gentle and attentive and promises not to be violent again. Walker's research suggests that as the cycle repeats, both phase one and phase three become shorter in duration; in other words, a violent relationship is likely to become more violent rather than less violent unless the cycle is interrupted.

Consequently, when violence or even the fear of violent reprisal is reported, it is important for the therapist to address it directly. It is generally valuable to develop a no-violence contract, to take effect immediately and to last until the next scheduled session. Although some therapists advocate getting an agreement in writing because doing so extracts another level of commitment, a verbal agreement is often sufficient.

To negotiate a no-violence contract, it is important to secure information that describes the evolution of the violence and its maintenance in the relationship. Walker's cycle of violence can be particularly helpful in guiding the information-gathering process. Determine what seems to provoke or establish conditions that can trigger the violent episodes. It can be very helpful to use the most recent incident as an example, since it will in all likelihood be representative of all the others. Have each partner describe, as specifically as possible, his or her behavior during each of the three phases. Once the specifics are identified, new options can be introduced to replace behaviors previously linked to violence. For instance, the husband who recognizes that each violent incident is preceded by a clenching of his jaws might be encouraged to use a time-out. The wife who comes to understand violence is preceded by changes in her own behavior (increased crying, for example) might use this perception to call a time-out.

Time-outs will not be very helpful, however, unless agreed-upon rules are attached to their use. For example, such a vaguely defined time-out as leaving the house may serve to escalate the incident if the partner left behind is jealous and wonders where the other is going and for how long. Useful time-out rules that can be negotiated during a session include no drug or alcohol use, agreed-upon people to be used as resources during the time-outs so as not to escalate a partner's jealousy, and means for communicating the amount of time needed on a specific occasion.

It is also valuable to have each spouse describe how the other can help curb behaviors identified as contributing to the violence. Developing this form of cooperation can help decrease the violent behavior, but the therapist must be sure to prohibit the violent spouse from holding the other responsible for his or her behavior. Individual responsibility and potential for self-control must be kept clearly in focus.

Finally, a no-violence contract needs to ensure physical safety of the spouse in danger of being physically hurt, who is usually, of course, the wife. Most communities have homes designated as safe houses, or shelters, for battered women. The use of this resource must be identified as a way the woman can not only care for herself, but aid the relationship as well. If this resource is not used, the violence can escalate to a point where the wife is seriously injured and the husband faces criminal charges. While the husband may not experience the wife as caring for the relationship at the time she uses this resource, establishing the shelter's importance beforehand and again when the crisis has passed can help prevent disaster.

Beyond negotiating the initial contract, it is also important that the therapist spend time in future sessions discussing the role of violence in relationships. Weitzman and Dreen (1982) have identified issues around which most battering couples become locked into rigidly complementary relationships with little room for negotiation. These issues include the regulation of distance and intimacy, jealousy and loyalty, dependence and independence, rejection and unconditional acceptance, adequacy and inadequacy, and power and powerlessness. It seems that most problems of battering couples are anchored in attempts to resolve one or more of these issues, which will eventually have to be addressed in therapy. For instance, Hoffman (1976) has discussed how violence can become a perverse way of developing periodic closeness in a relationship, followed by predictable distancing. In this sense, distance in the relationship comes to be regulated by the violence. The goal of therapy in such a case becomes regulation of distance in the relationship without reliance on violence. If this goal is not met, a separation or other form of treatment, such as the many groups for batterers and the battered, may also be needed. Regardless, it is important to keep communicating to all involved that no one deserves the ill will and shame that emanate from interpersonal violence—not to mention its potential for lasting physical harm. Violence is an issue that needs ongoing therapeutic attention.

≡ Reporting Sexual and Physical Abuse

Between 1963 and 1965 all fifty states passed laws requiring the reporting of sexual and physical abuse to the proper authorities. These laws vary from state to state, but typically carry stiff penalties in the form of fines, jail sentences, and/or professional sanctions. Therapists should familiarize themselves with the reporting laws and procedures in their jurisdiction as soon as they settle in a new locale. Learning about the laws is also a means of introducing the therapist to the protective service staff who are in a significant position to make referrals.

In consideration of these laws, it is incumbent upon the practicing therapist to report any incident within twenty-four hours of learning of the abuse, the period usually required by reporting laws. Although there is the concern about breaking confidentiality and the effects on the therapeutic relationship, the laws supersede confidentiality. Also, while the report will likely promote a crisis and result in inhibiting the therapeutic relationship for at least a short time, the resulting crisis can often serve to activate change in an abusive family that would otherwise not occur, or occur only after much time and suffering have passed. In this sense, as antithetical as it may appear, the reporting can often result in tremendous therapeutic value because change is promoted after the initial upheaval. The therapist reporting the abuse may not be in a position to render assistance, but may very well serve as the catalyst to "open" the family to the help of others.

Most states allow for the reporting of an abusive situation anonymously, but the family is probably best served by the therapist who tells them that signs of abuse will have to be reported and then attempts to process family reactions. Therapist candor in this situation can serve as a model of effective interpersonal behavior, which is so frequently absent in abusive families. Typically, these families are closed systems pervaded by secrets. In this regard, the therapist's openness and directness is often a new experience and one that can promote the rekindling of a positive therapeutic relationship once the initial trauma has been resolved. Regardless of what might happen, though, the therapist must report and must be prepared for the potential onslaught by the family and/or the therapist's own struggle with the issue of reporting. At these times it is important to remember that this type of crisis may be the only catalyst that can promote change for these families; it may be necessary to short-circuit the harm that may otherwise occur to the children.

For these reasons, therapists are wise to become acquainted with the area child protective services staff. Doing so can facilitate the reporting process and ensure the therapist of having more input into treatment recommendations for the family as well as an opportunity to encourage the protective services staff to acknowledge and implement a systems perspective. In this way, the family therapist can have a positive impact on the larger societal system that deals with abusive families.

≡ Dealing with Suicide Threats

Many families have been touched by suicide. Unfortunately, suicide has a dramatic ripple effect; the lives of relatives and friends are seriously damaged, in the form of emotional and mental disturbances, failure in life tasks, and repetition of suicide and other forms of self-destructive behavior.

When suicide is mentioned as an option by someone in the family, it must be taken seriously and responded to by the therapist. The activation of the family becomes crucial at this point, and family members should be tapped as resources. For instance, after a family member has identified suicide as an option, other family members can be asked: "You just heard Jack talk of killing himself as a way out of this. When pushed like he's feeling, it's not easy to think of all possible options. We all know suicide is a permanent solution to what is usually something that will subside or pass. In Jack's shoes, what do you believe are the other options available?" Once the family members offer what they believe to be the variety of options available, the person talking of suicide is asked to respond to the suggestions. Throughout this process the goal has a short-term focus of identifying not only possible options, but also ways in which each family member would be willing to help in this time of crisis. As with the options offered, the family member considering suicide is asked to identify what assistance offered by the family members he or she would like to receive.

Once this process is completed, a contract is negotiated for implementation between the current session and the next. The goal is to create a perception of the circumstances as manageable, to replace the suicidal person's notion of the world as out of control and no longer manageable. It is also important to recognize that a suicidal person's expression may be representative of other family members' thoughts and feelings as well. In this regard, it is valuable to ask each person about his or her experiences with suicidal thinking. Typically, at least one other person will acknowledge suicidal thoughts, and frequently most of the others will. The discovery of universality is often curative by itself. It also sets the tone for future treatment considerations regarding how the family members do not use one another as resources but instead hide and feel alone in despair.

Richman (1986) has identified a set of characteristics of a family in which suicide is a possibility. While most of these characteristics are reflective of dysfunctional families regardless of presenting problem, his observations and treatment ideas are worthy of attention. He identifies the following as characteristics of families with suicidal potential: an inability to accept necessary change, such as separations and mourning; role and interpersonal conflicts; disturbed family structure, such as fragility or prohibition of intimacy outside the family; one-sided intrafamilial relationships, such as scapegoating; affective difficulties, such as a one-sided pattern of aggression or a family depression; communication disturbances; and an intolerance for crises. The interested reader is referred to Richman's book for more detailed treatment considerations.

Many clinicians also ask potentially suicidal clients three questions: Have you attempted suicide before? If you were to kill yourself, how would you do it? Do you have the means (gun, pills, etc) ready? Because these three questions are the best predictors of suicide, a positive answer to all three may suggest short-term hospitalization. Also, as a result of asking these questions, the therapist can feel more assured that precautions were taken to prevent a suicide.

≡5≡ CASE MANAGEMENT PROCEDURES

INTRODUCTION

To manage families through the process of therapy effectively and to supply services in a professional manner, therapists need to know how to call on outside resources, how to get paid, how to keep notes, and how to perform a host of other case management aspects of family therapy. The procedures described in this chapter are meant to meet that need. Ordinarily, one begins to learn how to manage cases during the practicum phase of training. Unfortunately, the procedures developed in training clinics are not always applicable to the private practice or agency setting. Case management procedures evolve out of the needs of a particular setting. In this chapter we attempt to describe case management procedures that are applicable across settings.

TELLING CLIENTS ABOUT VACATION

Everyone needs a break in the routine of daily work, and family therapists are no different. The structure of therapy practice, however, interferes with that need because the right time for a vacation never seems to present itself. Within a group of clients, some family or another is always at a crucial phase in treatment, or some couple is always just about to make the flight to health. The problem is how to create the needed space in the appointment calendar without feeling irresponsible.

Clients can easily cope even if their therapist is on an extended vacation (more than two weeks) if they are warned well in advance and if they know what to do in a crisis. An upcoming vacation should be first mentioned approximately four sessions (weekly appointment schedule) beforehand and again at each session until the vacation begins. A statement such as "I want to let you know that I'll be out of town for three weeks beginning next month," or something similar, is adequate. Some therapists use the impending break as an intervention by asking clients to predict potential problems and crises and to discuss potential means of resolution. More typically, a long discussion of the upcoming break in sessions is not appropriate because the pace of therapy may be affected and any information regarding whom to call in a crisis may be forgotten.

In the following weeks, clients will need reminding, they will need information about whom to call in an emergency, and they will need to know the date of their next session after the break. Therapists in group practice often give clients the name and phone number of a colleague who has been briefed about the caseload. Those in solo practice may rely on a secretary, an answering service, or an answering machine to convey phone messages from clients needing emergency consultation. With the advent of voice mail systems, maintaining contact with the office while on vacation is becoming easier.

To avoid the difficulties imposed by extended vacations, many therapists take three- or four-day holidays instead. No warning is usually required because appointments can easily be shifted or cancelled for one week. True irresponsibility is not realizing the need to take time off in order to avoid getting burned out. Therapy is highly demanding of intellectual and emotional resources, and the burnout cost is equally demanding. We all know therapists who have sacrificed their health, their jobs, and ultimately their own families to duty and service. The cost of not taking time off is high; time off is part of the job.

ACCEPTING REFERRALS

Palazzoli-Selvini and her colleagues have stated, "The problem of the referring person in family therapy is one of the most insidious and potentially compromising to the success of treatment" (Palazzoli-Selvini et al., 1980, p.3). Nevertheless, the importance of the referring person to therapy needs to be considered. Frequently, the referring person may have become intimately involved in the family's organization and operation and, without realizing it, could prove to be a significant homeostatic force in family therapy. Palazzoli-Selvini finds that child psychiatrists, pediatricians, and family physicians commonly become referring persons after treating one family member for a long time and becoming a friend of the family in the process. Consequently, it is important that the family therapist ascertain the role and function of the referring person in the family's life. Often, this can be expedited by inviting the referring person to the first session. During this session, prior involvements and a history can be secured, and, more importantly, future roles, expectations, and means of communicating can be established and agreed upon by all. The referring person's ongoing involvement with the family, assuming this is to be the case, can be identified as the family therapist delineates responsibility and goals for the person's involvement.

If the referring person is a therapist, it is valuable to determine from him or her and from the family what has been attempted that was helpful and what has proven ineffective. This can provide the family therapist valuable information about what might be most beneficial to attempt. Also, it is good to find out why the referral is being made now, as opposed to some other time. For example, is the referral being made out of frustration/anger with the family (another family therapist making the referral because of this family's apparent unwillingness to effect change that appears within their reach), or is the referring person suggesting that the family's needs appear too challenging (the neurologist who has been treating a brain-damaged family member or the child psychologist who has been doing play therapy with the child)? Whatever the reason for the referral, it must be considered in light of the referring person's prior involvement.

Once the referral has been made and therapy is progressing, sending the referring person a letter of thanks that also contains a brief note regarding the family's status is always valuable. Recognize that in some cases, the referring person may be more involved and need to be asked to rejoin therapy at future points, which would lessen the need for this type of letter.

MAKING REFERRALS

The following constitute situations that can precipitate a referral to another therapist: (1) the therapist or family is relocating, (2) the client(s) presents a unique problem requiring that a different orientation or specialty become clinically involved, or (3) the therapist and/or family determine they are unable to negotiate a viable therapeutic contract.

When the therapist or family is relocating and together they determine there is value in continued therapeutic involvement, a referral will usually be provided by the therapist. If the therapist is relocating, the therapist can usually make a sound referral based upon firsthand knowledge of the colleague to whom the referral is being made. Even in this case there is real value in having at least one session, prior to the original therapist's departure in which the therapist and family meet with the new therapist. Such a meeting provides the opportunity to review prior involvements, goals, and what has and has not been helpful and to discuss future goals and directions. Referring in this fashion tends to diminish the clients' sense of having "something done to them" and their concern for what is being said about them outside of sessions.

When the family is relocating, therapists can either utilize their professional network to identify possible therapists in the family's new locale or help the family by identifying how they might go about locating a competent therapist. A professional network such as that provided by the American Association for Marriage and Family Therapy (AAMFT) or the American Family Therapy Association (AFTA) can be immensely helpful in this regard. Even if personal information is not available about therapists in the family's new locale, membership in organizations such as these can be one criterion they can be encouraged to use. They can also be encouraged to visit therapists who may be suggested to them by coworkers, neighbors, clergy, or the family doctor and determine if they feel comfortable with one of those recommended.

During the last session it is also wise to have clients sign a release-of-information form that authorizes release of clinical notes once they relocate. In fact, we have found it very helpful to use the last session or even two to have the family discuss the essence of what would be related to a new therapist. They are asked to address things such as goals achieved and those not yet achieved but hoped for, what they have done to achieve the goals, how the therapist was most helpful, and what they would have liked more or less of in the therapy. This procedure not only helps to facilitate the transition, but also provides another means of reinforcing the contents and results of their therapeutic process.

There are also those times when the family's problem is outside the professional interest or expertise of the therapist. An example might be the family that presents with an adolescent who is eating disordered to a therapist who has not been successful with this type of problem in the past but who knows of an area agency or therapist who specializes in this type of problem. In fact, faced with this type of situation, we believe the therapist is ethically bound to make a referral.

Other types of specific presenting problems that therapists may regard as sufficiently outside their expertise to necessitate a referral are those families with an alcoholic, with a specific sexual dysfunction, with difficulty adapting to a particular disability such as mental retardation, or with a parent sexually abused as a child who is now the agent of reported incest. While cases such as those just cited may necessitate the referral of the entire family or couple to another therapist, there are some that may suggest a referral of an individual in the family to another therapist or group available in the area. A prime example might be a family in which one of the parents is the child of an alcoholic, and the therapist may want to refer that person to an area group for adult children of alcoholics. The learning that person secures from the group can then be intentionally incorporated into the family work.

Most therapists acknowledge that they cannot engage all families or couples productively. While there is always value for the therapist in employing introspection, consultation, and interaction with the family to solicit feedback for learning in this area, there will likely be some people with whom a therapist just does not "connect," and a referral will become necessary. In these cases therapists are ethically responsible for facilitating as effective a referral as can be carried out. Certainly, therapists also have a responsibility for being candid and ensuring that feelings such as anger and frustration are not displaced onto the family.

INTRODUCING A NEW COTHERAPIST

A cotherapist may be introduced into the therapeutic system or may replace one who is leaving. In either case the occurrence can be a vital occasion as a source of new energy becomes available to the participants.

The transition from one cotherapist to the next is facilitated by having at least one session at which both are present. This provides the family and departing cotherapist an opportunity to say goodbye, and the new cotherapist can participate in the experience and use it as a means of sharing something important with the family prior to initiating the therapeutic relationship. This time can also be used to identify accomplishments for the new member and as an opportunity to underscore and/or revise the therapeutic contract. This change can in fact have a significant impact in revitalizing ongoing therapy.

There are also occasions when the therapist may choose to be joined by a cotherapist. This may be done for a multitude of reasons, such as becoming "stuck" with a family and wanting new input, facilitating the training/supervisory process of a therapist, or choosing as a matter of personal preference to function with a cotherapist when none has been previously available. During the first session with a cotherapist in attendance, there is value in encouraging the couple/family to share their perceptions of prior work. This provides the cotherapist with the opportunity of determining the clients' perceptions of therapy to that point; it also provides the family another occasion to reaffirm publicly what they have accomplished and to reshape the direction of therapy should their review suggest it. This is also a time for the cotherapist to identify his or her style of working and how they hope to be helpful, based upon what was learned from the clients.

During the get acquainted period it is important for the new cotherapist to monitor his or her own ego needs and not be offended should the family members appear to be more attentive to their "old" therapist. Certainly this phenomenon is not an unusual one, and it is best to expect this behavior initially. Should the new cotherapist attempt to overcompensate and push himself or herself on the family, the long-term effects could be detrimental. The original therapist can facilitate this transition by initially being attentive to the cotherapist, addressing him or her frequently, asking for his or her perceptions, and generally demonstrating respect and value. In most cases this will serve as a catalyst for the family's quick acceptance of a new cotherapist.

INTRODUCING A CONSULTING PROFESSIONAL

There are times when the practicing family therapist may want to introduce a consultant to the therapeutic system. Examples are when (1) a family presents concern for a child's learning problems and a psychologist may be introduced to do an assessment, or (2) the family therapist may feel stuck and want to introduce a consultant for one or two sessions to provide new insight and impetus to the therapy. Naturally, these two reasons may also be combined, as when a family presents itself with a member who is concerned about having been sexually abused as a child, is possibly drug dependent, or has some other problem that would prompt the family therapist to introduce a consultant. With these cases the consultant might be present to provide new information and to be productively provocative to the therapeutic effort. The reasons for introducing a consultant, then, are to provide new information to the therapeutic system and/or a new component to the system that will result, one hopes, in dislodging barriers and promoting renewed movement.

When choosing the consultant, regardless of the reason, it is important for the therapist to decide if the family should be involved in this process. In those cases involving couples or families who present themselves as dependent and reactive in nature, or with those clients who seem only tenuously engaged in the therapeutic process, it seems best to empower them by involving them in making the decision about a consultant. Families that have been involved in therapy and are emotionally engaged and committed to the process need not become involved in the decision-making process. There is value, however, in informing them of the consultant's background and how his or her role is perceived in the treatment plan.

Attributing expert status to the consultant often increases the potential for effecting change. The fact that the consultant is from outside the therapeutic system also provides an increased potential for therapeutic leverage. The family knows that an "outsider" will not have the same vested interests in something being said as those they might attribute to their regular therapist. This situation also puts the therapist in the unusual position of siding with the family against what the consultant might say; it therefore strengthens the therapeutic alliance while still making important new information available for therapy. For instance, the consultant who says to the family "I do not see any evidence of you really wanting to change" can be disagreed with, and the ongoing therapist will be in a different position in relation to the family while still promoting their therapeutic movement. As the ongoing therapist disagrees with the now departed consultant, comments can be uttered such as the following:

> "I do not agree with him and it irritates me that he did not show more understanding and concern for you folks." (This tends to emphasize the understanding and concern of the ongoing therapist.)

> "I believe you demonstrate many characteristics reflective of a desire to change, but I wonder if they are evident only to us and may appear disguised to outsiders." (This statement, among other things, serves to tighten the sense of the therapist and family being together in this.)

> "Do you have some ideas on how you might disguise your desire to change?" (This question is designed to provoke the family to begin to explore their elements of change and how they may not be fully capitalizing on these resources.)

Consultants can be a rich source of catalyzing changes with couples and families. Consultants may be experts on some particular issue (alcoholism, incest) or a colleague from down the hall who will provide a much needed new perspective. Regardless, consultation is a resource that is probably not used nearly as often as its value would merit.

DISCUSSING FEES WITH CLIENTS

Fees for services rendered are a fact of life and should be dealt with directly by the family therapist. Many believe that therapists who have fees handled by a receptionist are missing out on a potentially valuable therapeutic opportunity. If the couple/family has insurance that pays for the service, the receptionist can likely handle the necessary paperwork, but there is much value in the therapist's handling those situations in which the clients pay directly for the service.

One way of handling fee payment is to tell the clients that they can pay at the end of every session or after every other session, as they might choose. This option not only gives them the element of choice, it also guards against the generation of bills so large that they create animosity in either the therapist or clients. If an unpaid bill is left to grow, it is not unreasonable to expect that the therapist and clients may begin to experience ill will toward one another, particularly at times of painful but necessary confrontation or when a therapeutic plateau seems to have been reached. Consequently, keeping the bill regularly paid up should be regarded as a preventive measure designed to avoid problems.

When therapists handle their own fees, they are also afforded a direct opportunity to model for clients how to consider oneself important and communicate directly and openly about issues that may be regarded as sensitive by others. In all likelihood, these issues of self-esteem and communication about sensitive material are difficulties for at least some family members. The negotiation of fee payments thus allows the therapist an opportunity to immediately model and begin to address structural issues of therapy. This technique also provides the therapist the opportunity to observe how decisions are made in the family. Do they consult one another, or does one member make the decision unilaterally? Also, who seems to be responsible for the management of money?

Making exceptions in the matter of payment of fees is often a harbinger of erosion of the therapist's effectiveness and the family's sense of engagement in the therapy. Although various reasons might be offered for these occurrences, the important consideration in this regard is to prevent erosion by not becoming lax. Unfortunately, therapists have not attended to this issue as directly as its importance should dictate. It is discussed only rarely in the professional literature and training programs, and it seems to have been given an aura of forbidden mystery. Until therapists value themselves enough to address fees directly, it may be unrealistic to expect more respect from society as a whole.

ASSESSING WHEN A FAMILY IS TOO DEPENDENT

While the therapist is concerned with developing a therapeutic alliance sufficient to effect change, there is also a need to ensure that the family does not become too dependent. Signs of problematic dependency might become evident in the form of phone calls between sessions to receive confirmation of particular ideas or perceptions, requests for sessions more frequently than what the therapist deems appropriate, or comments made in session such as "We agreed that we would wait to discuss this until we were here and you could tell us if we were right."

With couples or families who make frequent phone calls between sessions, a simple prescription is often effective. They are instructed that the next time they feel disposed to call and report an incident or ask a question, they are to wait twenty-four hours from the moment of the initial impulse before calling. If the desire is still present at the end of that period of time, they are to call; otherwise, they are to make note of the incident and report it in the next session. Most frequently, they already have the answer to their question or ideas about possible solutions to an incident and are simply looking for affirmation or approval rather than relying upon their internal resources. In the vast majority of situations their ideas and solutions are appropriate. The situations they might otherwise call about will typically require some action within twenty-four hours, and asking them to be responsive to a twenty-four-hour phone moratorium increases the likelihood that they will implement their own ideas.

When these incidents are reported in the next session, it is important for the therapist to recognize the nature of the clients' actions and to emphasize the positives that are inherent in what they did. On those occasions when they do call after the twenty-four-hour moratorium, it is wise to ask what they have been thinking about doing and encourage them to select from among the options they have identified: "It seems you are definitely on the right track and have thought of good options." In the next scheduled session it will be important to reinforce the clients for the insight they have manifested in regard to the situation presented on the phone and underscore it as evidence of the progress they have made.

Dependence might also be evidenced when the therapist states the belief that it is appropriate to consider less frequent sessions and/or termination, and the couple/family responds by requesting maintenance of the same schedule or even more frequent sessions. In these circumstances there is value in asking clients what they are uneasy about. As they describe their fears and apprehensions, the therapist listens and determines how these uneasy situations develop and what can be done to prevent them from occurring.

There is also value in having them identify what is the worst that could happen if their fears materialize. Once their worst fears are identified, the therapist is wise to explore with them options for action in response to these developments. Oftentimes this discussion will serve to ease their apprehensions; if not, they should be encouraged to "give it a try" and then implement the options they just discussed.

There may even be times when there is value in encouraging clients to attempt to develop one of these uncomfortable or fearful situations to practice implementing the various options identified. This suggestion serves to take the edge off of their apprehension and allows the therapist to metacommunicate a sense of conviction and belief in the clients that they may not otherwise have in themselves.

Those who appear to be manifesting problematic dependence by frequently reporting the decision to wait until they were in session to discuss an issue or to get feedback should be encouraged to talk about the issue at that time while the therapist observes. This serves to desensitize discussing issues to resolution, and it also provides the therapist with an opportunity to observe communication styles on issues that clients perceive as sensitive. By intervening at the process level of their communication, the therapist can facilitate the development of skills and resources that result in clients' feeling more competent and less restricted, and subsequently less dependent upon the therapist as a mediator or insurance policy against the total destruction about which they may be apprehensive.

WHEN TO TERMINATE

The issue of termination in family therapy is not nearly so crucial an issue as it is portrayed to be when working from an individual perspective. Family therapy is oriented to facilitating family members' coming to use one another, rather than the therapist, as primary resources. The notion of cure is not nearly as prominent in family therapy as it is with individuals, because families are continually evolving through a life cycle with predictably difficult times and because of family therapy's tendency to be more problem-specific than is most individual therapy.

One way of reducing, if not eliminating, the issue of termination is to work on the basis of specific temporal boundaries. From the outset of therapy, there is agreement among all involved that therapy will last for a certain number of sessions. If the agreement is to meet for five sessions, it is understood that everyone, including the therapist, will decide if they have accomplished the goals by the fifth session and then enter into a decision-making process about the value/need of negotiating for more sessions to reach a particular goal. If an agreement to continue is reached, the purpose and time frame is once again agreed upon. As a result, everyone gains a temporal orientation similar to those to which we have grown accustomed in daily life: watches on almost everyone's arm, clocks on many walls, calendars distributed liberally at the start of each year, and pocket calendars in purses and vest pockets. There is a feeling of comfort, if not security, in having some sense of time—and the same holds true for therapy.

At the end of each negotiated time period, the therapist can facilitate the discussion about continuing with another "treatment block of time" and/or encourage clients to go home and discuss continuing and then contact the therapist with a decision. Should they call and desire to continue, there is value for the therapist in asking them to explain not only what area of change or goal they wish to achieve, but also how they decided. Frequently, the description of how they decided to continue suggests termination because they have demonstrated the capability of operating in very independent and functional ways. If the therapist agrees to continue, it is understood to be for a time-limited period once again.

Working on the basis of these temporally specified treatment blocks significantly minimizes the issue of termination and provides everyone with recognizable times when it is easy to terminate. It is not unreasonable to assume some families may develop a loyalty and liking for the therapist that makes termination uncomfortable enough for them to postpone. While some might suggest that this is an indication of the family's need for more "work," it is incumbent upon the therapist to make it easy for the family to exercise free choice in ending *their* therapy, for most assuredly it should be theirs.

Families may give other clues of their desire to terminate by not showing up for scheduled appointments or asking questions such as, "Do you think we're accomplishing anything here?" or "We've been talking among ourselves about coming only once a month rather than every other week. What do you think about that?" When these and other such behaviors that may suggest the family's readiness to terminate are present, there is generally value in offering to terminate rather than going to greater spacing between sessions. This way it can become the family's free decision in response to the therapist's invitation, and they can also sense the therapist's autonomy from them and the fact that there is no dependency or urgency in continuing on the therapist's part. It is still possible for the family to suggest greater spacing of sessions rather than outright termination, but at least the invitation/permission for them to terminate will have been given. Regardless of whether they decide to terminate or opt for greater spacing of sessions, it is advisable to explore with them likely struggles or tensions in the future so that when normal crises or tensions arise, they do not attribute this directly to the decision to terminate.

At the point of termination there can be value in suggesting another session in two to four months. While a followup session can facilitate the termination process for the family, it can also be a rich source of data for the therapist. By seeing families after two to four months, the therapist can assess the effectiveness of various interventions over a period of time and enrich his or her experiential base regarding what is helpful to families with various presenting problems. This practice is one way of preventing therapist burnout resulting from an absence of feedback on the effectiveness of various practices.

KEEPING USABLE NOTES

Historically, clinical case notes have been more content oriented than process oriented. Process notes are more specific regarding systemic notions such as the family's rules, roles, evident communication styles, and patterns that appear to be operational. Attending to the organization and structure of a family in notes lends itself to the development of direction, goals, and possible interventions for the therapist. Merely recording the content of who said what and where the session left off ignores such systemic information and may, in fact, get in the way of the therapist's appropriately conceptualizing the family in a systemic fashion. We can all be entranced and diverted by stories. Clinical notes that focus on content are typically more reflective of stories than the workings of the people involved.

The therapist who functions with a particular internalized model for conceptualizing families will often find case notes referring to that model particularly useful. For instance, following the model for conceptualizing family functioning presented by Lewis, Beavers, Gossett, and Phillips (1976) lends itself nicely to process-oriented notes that naturally lead to therapeutic directions or goals. This model has specific checkpoints or potential issues built in, such as: Are parental coalitions present or absent? Is the family chaotically organized, organized by dominance, or egalitarian? Are there vague and indistinct boundaries among family members or disengagement that results in members' questioning the sense of being connected? Are they verbally invasive of one another? Can they manifest a sense of openness to one another's perceptions, or are they impermeable in this respect? Notes that are geared to a model of this nature will prove to have the most utilitarian value and be most likely to facilitate successful change if included with information such as who attended the session, any out-of-session assignments, or other case management details.

TAKING A BREAK DURING A SESSION

Where is it written that therapy sessions are to last a certain number of minutes and that no break is to be taken during the session? Even Freud was reported to interrupt analytic sessions for a visit to the bathroom (Meisel & Kendrick, 1985). The answer to the question is obvious; the routines we establish as service providers are learned, usually without question, from our mentors and they from theirs. The therapy session without a break is one such custom, not the product of research.

Family therapists have been willing to abandon traditional practice customs and establish service routines that better fit the needs of their clients. Families are often seen for longer than the typical one-hour individual session once each week. Many authors have recommended 1½-hour sessions for married couples and two- to three-hour sessions for large families (billing rates by the hour). Along with these longer sessions, however, comes increased client and therapist fatigue.

The initial session, when the therapist presents an overview of what therapy will be like, is a good time to state that short breaks will be taken.

Then before the next session begins, the family can be reminded that a break will be taken at some time during the session. When the therapist notices fatigue creeping in, a simple statement such as "Let's take a five-minute break," delivered at a transition point in the session, will suffice.

As a result of changes in session time span, rest breaks are not the only kinds of breaks used by family therapists. Because longer sessions have meant that therapists have more information to process during a session, a few minutes spent away from the distraction of clients can be very helpful in collecting thoughts, reviewing, and reorienting session plans. There is absolutely nothing inappropriate in a therapist stating, "I need to collect my thoughts, so I'll step out for a few minutes. In the meantime, I would like you to . . . ." In this directive statement, the clients are given a task while the therapist takes a break, and the message is clear that they are to keep working.

Changes in treatment methods also have led to the need to take breaks during sessions. The therapy team approach in which the therapist(s) and a group of observers work together requires that a communication link between the two be established. Although technological aids such as the telephone and bug-in-the-ear serve this need quite well, there are times that the therapist and the observers need to get together face to face during a session, and a rest break or therapist break can provide that opportunity.

When the therapist steps out of the session with the sole purpose of consulting with the observing team, the clients should be given several messages. The statement "I'm going to consult with the team. I'll be back in a few minutes. I'd like you to continue talking about . . . ." will tell clients why the therapist is leaving and what they are to do in the meantime. Helping clients understand why the therapist is leaving prevents their misinterpretation of the break. It also forewarns clients that the therapist may come back to the session and deliver a message from the team or radically change the direction of the session. Without such an implied warning, the "doctrine of no surprises" may be violated and the therapist may feel awkward and hesitant either to deliver a message from the team or to change tactics in a session. Giving the clients a task helps keep the mood or theme of a session intact. The therapist can leave and come back without feeling disruptive and, as a result, consult with the team when necessary.

Taking breaks is a common feature of family therapy. With attention given to timing and the way breaks are initiated, fatigue can be relieved, a therapist can gain the opportunity to review and reorient the session process, and colleagues can be consulted.

≡ 6 ≡ SELF- AND COTHERAPIST MANAGEMENT

INTRODUCTION

Only a small portion of the family therapy literature is devoted to the effects of therapy on those who practice it. Topics such as burnout and ethical dilemmas have received attention. Few experienced therapists, however, have written openly about their feelings of being bored or stuck in sessions, their dislike for some clients, and the full range of other human emotions and problems that are part of any service occupation. Such feelings and problems do indeed exist, and coping strategies have been developed. The collection of procedures in this chapter pertains to how family therapists manage themselves in dealing with the rigors of the job.

FEELING SEXUALLY ATTRACTED TO A CLIENT

Sexual exploitation of clients by therapists has become a widely publicized concern in both the professional and lay literature. This form of abuse is one that all therapists should particularly avoid in view of the vulnerability typically experienced by clients in the therapist-client relationship. To underscore professional ethics codes, more and more states are legislating and imposing stiff criminal penalties for therapists who choose to exploit clients in this way.

Assuming behavior is generally preceded by a feeling state, therapists are wise to be responsive to feelings of sexual attraction to a client. While these feelings may not culminate in sexual acting out, they certainly could clutter professional objectivity and reduce the potential for being helpful.

Suppose, for instance, that a therapist is attracted to the wife of a couple being seen. If this physical attraction is not addressed, it may lead the therapist to become overprotective of the wife in session, or it may take another form and lead to an attack on her directly and/or to overly identify and side with her husband. Neither of these options will be therapeutic for either of the partners or their therapy. For this reason, it is important for the therapist to have supervision available at these times so that attraction feelings can be professionally processed and monitored to ensure the best possible service for the clients.

Along with concern for the clients' welfare, feelings of sexual attraction to clients (particularly if they occur frequently) may be reflective of a dynamic within the therapist that constitutes a psychological blind spot, which will not be resolved without the benefit of supervision and/or therapy.

FEELING BORED WITH A CASE/SESSION

Therapists, like other people, periodically experience boredom. For this reason, it is important for therapists to be certain that what they interpret as boredom with a case is not emanating from their own world and not being displaced onto clients. Assuming there is no reason to believe that what is being experienced as boredom is primarily the therapist's responsibility, there can be value in using these feelings therapeutically. Therapists may use these sensations to ask themselves: How have we become stalemated? In what way has our therapeutic system become like their relationship? In what ways am I, or are we, playing it safe and consequently just experiencing sameness with little potential for initiating change? What may I be perceiving in their relationship that is uncomfortable for me in my own life and subsequently defending against by avoiding a therapeutic confrontation? What needs to be confronted/addressed that I am missing? These questions can be best addressed with the assistance of a colleague or supervisor facilitating the exploration with the therapist.

Carl Whitaker and some of the Italian family therapists, such as Andolfi, have discussed the utilization of boredom as a therapeutic ally. They suggest presenting the boredom to the couple or family and encouraging them to take initiative to reengage the therapist. This tactic is based upon the supposition that the couple or family feels some sense of allegiance and/or commitment to the therapist and the therapeutic process. Without a sense of attachment, it is reasonable to assume the family would interpret this suggestion from the therapist as rejection or apathy and choose to terminate therapy. When there is a question about the intensity of their commitment, it is advisable to assume some potential ownership in describing the boredom. For instance:

> I've been thinking about our recent session(s). As I have reflected on it I don't know if it's me or what, but it's been difficult for me to be as attentive as I like to be. It's as though what has been being addressed doesn't seem to be vital or have much importance; it's as though we're beseiged with boredom. Like I say, perhaps it's just me, I'm not certain and that's the reason I'd like to discuss this with you now. What are your thoughts on this?

At other times, when there is some certainty regarding the therapeutic alliance and the nature of the relationship, it may suffice to simply say, "I find this boring and difficult to maintain an interest. For me, I need a change here to make sure I stay involved the way I want to be."

Regardless of which of these suggestions might be followed, the wise therapist will be responsive to boredom that is experienced and not just attempt to disregard it. To do so could be very dangerous and a big step in the direction of burning out both professionally and personally.

FEELING STUCK IN A SESSION

Family therapy is a complex process, and even the most competent therapist does not always know which procedure in a session will prove to be the most beneficial. What has been successful in the past may or may not succeed again, and what has failed before may yield striking gains. A chesslike strategy, in which every move is planned on the basis of many possible countermoves, is an impossible dream in the context of therapy. As a result of this lack of predictability, therapists must expect to feel stumped, confused, and stuck.

More specifically, getting stuck means losing contact with what is happening or becoming overwhelmed with all the options of intervening in the session so that no action is taken. For example, when clients are allowed to drone on and on about a specific issue, therapists often allow their concentration to drift. Then, when the client stops speaking, a momentary silence occurs because the therapist has not kept up with the discussion. It is in this lull that feelings of being stuck can be most pronounced.

Getting unstuck typically requires that the therapist do something different from what he or she has been doing. If, for instance, the therapist is stuck in an empathic responding mode and is unable to think far enough ahead of the client (the client makes short statements) to do anything other than reflect, the simple acts of standing up, changing chairs, or stretching while sitting can provide the opportunity for redirection of the session and a transition to another topic. Becoming unstuck is mostly the product of providing your mind with the opportunity to consider new options. Altering physical position and taking a five-minute break are easily implemented changes that can create such opportunities.

BUILDING CLIENT CONFIDENCE IN THERAPIST ABILITY

The best way to establish rapport with clients is to be helpful. For too long therapists have thought that rapport needs to be established prior to being helpful, rather than recognizing that being effective and helpful is the best means of establishing rapport. An important initial step in being helpful is to project an image of confidence and competence. The business world has attended to this issue through various publications on how to dress, shake hands, maintain eye contact, and decorate an office correctly. While all these factors likely play a role in projecting competence and facilitating development of the client's sense of confidence, the therapist can also engage in specific behaviors that further this development.

The therapist can make statements such as the following to facilitate confidence development. After a couple has initially described their circumstances, the therapist can say, "Your situation is one I am very familiar with. I have seen many couples, particularly in the recent past, with almost identical situations, and they have been very successful in securing the change they wanted." This statement communicates that their circumstance is not a new one for the therapist and also conveys a sense of hope. Naturally, the therapist needs to be careful of overdoing this to a point that the couple feels misunderstood because their "uniqueness" is disqualified.

Another way of inspiring confidence is to anticipate what clients are thinking, but have not yet spoken, and then say it for them. For instance, consider the couple in which the wife is disturbed about her husband's drinking and identifies herself as the adult child of an alcoholic, abusive father. She has just finished a detailed explanation of her disturbance secondary to the husband's drinking. The therapist might anticipate what the husband is thinking and address him by saying, "Bill, I imagine as you listen to your wife you find yourself wondering how much of Betty's concern is really attributable to you and how much of her concern is the residual of having been raised with her alcoholic father. You wonder about the fairness of it all." He will likely be quick to agree and attribute some degree of competence to the therapist for understanding his situation. Further, similar anticipations can be stated about Betty's thoughts in response to Bill's agreement. For instance, a therapist might say to her, "And Betty, I would suppose you perceive his agreement with what I'm suggesting as further evidence of how he is just like your father with all the denial and projection of responsibility." These efforts at speculating about what spouses are thinking or feeling in the initial stages of therapy can quickly foster clients' sense of confidence in the therapist.

Accepting what clients present without overt signs of being shocked or overwhelmed is another way of developing client confidence in the therapist. Being visibly overwhelmed or aghast by what is presented will likely promote alarm for the couple or family as they wonder if their therapist is up to the task of working with them. Although some families may benefit from the therapist's amplifying his or her affect (Minuchin, 1974), or dramatizing it, particularly in the early stages of therapy, most families benefit from perceiving their therapist as calmly accepting and attempting to completely understand what is presented.

≡ Client Questions the Therapist's Life Experience

Occasionally, some clients will question the credibility of the therapist on the basis of insufficient or inadequate life experience. This concern may be voiced in the form of questioning the therapist's apparent youth, status as an unmarried person, or lack of experience in raising children. Whatever the concern, the therapist should keep in mind the value of not reacting defensively to the client's inquiry. Keep in mind that the inquiry may be a legitimate one, and not necessarily an expression of resistance. Regardless of the client's motivation, it is likely that a defensive reaction by the therapist will not benefit the therapeutic relationship. Instead, the therapist should use the following type of response:

> That is a reasonable question on your part. I believe you and I will get along fine, because I also tend to be a wary consumer and like to know something about the product I'm buying before I leap in. You are right in assuming I'm [younger than you, have not raised children, etc.], but I do believe I can be of some assistance to you. My training has allowed me to acquire skills and knowledge designed to help you folks determine how you can develop more productive ways of operating, and I know I have been able to be helpful to others in situations similar to yours. In this same respect, I've worked with those who have eating disorders, those who were drug dependent, and those who were diagnosed as being psychotic. While I have never personally encountered any of these experiences, I do believe I have been able to be helpful to these folks.

I'd like for you to let me know how you think I'm doing as we move along, and I feel comfortable that you'll do so, recognizing you had enough foresight and wisdom to ask this question. Clients often have questions such as this, but never take the risk of asking. I appreciate your doing so. Also, keep in mind you are the employer here, and I the employee, so you can always terminate our contract should you decide.

Might you have any other questions at this time? God only knows, I ask more than my fair share.

This type of response will generally serve to allay whatever anxieties the clients might have, while also serving to solidify the therapeutic alliance rather than distancing it, as a defensive reaction probably would. Specifically, it also reinforces the clients by praising them for asking questions instead of sitting and ruminating about some issue and not attending to the business at hand. Just as important as the content of the therapist's response is the style in which it is delivered. Interpreting the question as a personal assault on professionalism, or whatever, will probably lead to a style of delivery that will override the desired effect of the content of the response. If the delivery style is haughty or defensive, it could at a minimum confuse the client, if not result in outright antagonism and escalation.

≡ Client Questions the Value of Therapy

There are times when clients question the value of their therapy. Their apprehensiveness may be expressed directly to the therapist, or it may be offered by one spouse reporting what the other spouse has said between sessions. When a spouse reports what the other has said, it will frequently be offered in the fashion of tattling as if in attempt to secure a more favorable position with the therapist or to belittle the other spouse. When this situation occurs, it is often valuable to try to neutralize the process by saying something such as: "I'm glad to hear that. I highly regard those clients who question and give consideration to their therapy. Frequently, I find they are the ones who benefit the most. In fact, I too have had some questions about what we have been doing, and perhaps this is a good time for us to discuss our concerns." While this serves to neutralize the tattler it also can serve as a convenient catalyst to discussing the course and process of therapy, which might otherwise be ignored.

This is a valuable time to question the goals of therapy, and the progress that has occurred in reaching them. Frequently, new goals will emanate from these discussions, as will valuable feedback for the therapist regarding the impact of various interventions that have been initiated so far. This corrective feedback can be applied to therapy with future clients.

A primary concern for the family therapist at these times is to avoid retreating into a defensive posture and counterattacking. The therapist whose ego is too invested in the work of therapy and is too reliant upon client approval is particularly vulnerable. Obviously, this type of behavior will not prove productive for anyone involved.

CLIENT THREATENS TO SUE FOR MALPRACTICE

One of the major fears clinicians in practice must face is the potential for a malpractice suit. Even though the chances of being sued are slim and the chances of a successful suit even slimmer, we must know how to deal with clients who for whatever reason are angry at their therapist and act out that anger through the threat of malpractice action.

Most typically, clients' feelings of anger are not the product of single instances when a therapist perhaps makes a mistake. Clients most often get angry as a result of a series of events or when issues have had a chance to build. For example, if a therapist allows clients to pay for sessions on a monthly or bimonthly basis, the risk of their getting angry about high therapy bills is much higher than if they paid by the session. Similarly, consider the client who threatens to sue because marital therapy ended in divorce. The divorce may have been a long time coming, with or without therapeutic intervention, and a client may blame a therapist to avoid personal responsibility. Typically, then, client threats to sue are predictable responses that can be foreseen.

Part of our job as therapists is to help clients face their feelings honestly. When clients seem to be withdrawing and letting themselves build toward anger, the therapist must open up discussion about the issue or issues of concern. For example, if a client is behind in paying fees, that issue should be openly discussed, and the sooner the better. Similarly, if a client appears angry, the therapist needs to initiate the discussion of what he or she is angry about. Beginning these discussions most often consists of an opener such as "We need to talk about your paying for the past three sessions," or "I sense you are irritated or angry at me about . . . . I would like to know what's bothering you because I'm getting worried."

The conversation following these openers can be made more productive if the clinician attends to the client's feelings. The important task in these discussions is open disclosure of feelings because open disclosure prevents the client from being forced to sue to get even, that is, to be taken seriously. The therapeutic skill most likely to prevent clients from carrying out a threat of malpractice action is empathic responding in a most Rogerian manner while simultaneously maintaining one's personal and professional integrity.

PRESESSION PLANNING

For every therapist who advocates extensive presession planning, another can be found who discounts value in this activity and may even consider it responsible for diminishing spontaneity. Practically speaking, there are legitimate arguments on both sides of this issue. There is value in considering patterns evident in a family's presentation and determining the most appropriate interventions at a particular point in time. On the other hand, spontaneity can be destroyed if the therapist enters the session with a plan that is quickly dashed by the family when they present a new crisis that does not fit with the plan.

Regardless of what position the therapist might have in relation to this issue, some basics do seem imperative. Minimally, the therapist should review past notes to keep current with the specifics of the case so that references can be made in therapy to what has occurred in the past. The therapist who never seems to remember what has occurred in the past will quickly be perceived as not regarding clients as important as we all like to feel. When the therapist periodically refers to what has been presented in past sessions, clients develop a sense of being valued and special. Similarly, review of past notes increases the potential of a therapist's identifying recurring themes or patterns in a family's presentation and subsequently developing the most appropriate interventions.

Most family therapists utilize out-of-session assignments at least periodically. Assuming a family is being seen for one hour per week, there are 167 hours available between sessions; homework can capitalize on these hours and serve as a catalyst to what happens in the weekly session. The presession planning period can serve to remind the therapist what homework might have been assigned and to ensure that the results of that assignment are checked out in the approaching session. The therapist who forgets to check out the results of assigned work runs the high risk of communicating to the family that homework assignments are "really not that important." As a result, it is likely that a family will be less responsive to future assigned tasks as they come to perceive them with the same degree of casualness as does their therapist.

MEETING CLIENTS OUTSIDE OF THERAPY

Meeting clients outside of therapy is bound to occur on occasion. However, in smaller communities there will likely be more frequent encounters. Therapists are wise not to promote discussion of issues that are, or have been, part of the therapy. During cross-examination the wise attorney avoids asking a question that could yield a harmful answer. Similarly, on meeting a client in the general community a therapist could open a Pandora's box of problems by asking questions. The answer may divulge information that places the therapist in a compromised position with regard to other family members and/or may result in the client's detaining the therapist for a long period of time.

On the occasion of these chance meetings it is advisable to keep the conversation as brief and casual as possible. Even while wanting to be sociable, the therapist should model appropriate maintenance of private time and personal boundaries. Should a particular client seem to be pressing for more than what the therapist is willing to offer at that time and context, a comment such as the following generally suffices: "It appears this is important, but speaking personally, I am not comfortable discussing this type of important information in this setting and under these time constraints. I would be far more comfortable if we were to pursue this issue in our next session. You deserve better than this." If it is a client seen in the past who is no longer involved in therapy, a similar comment encouraging him or her to call you to arrange another appointment should prove sufficient.

Therapists run the risk of burning out rapidly and beginning to resent their clients if they are not protective of their personal boundaries and are willing to engage clients wherever and whenever they meet. Such therapists might also be wise to reevaluate how they are perceiving themselves as professionals and ask themselves whether they may be attempting to satisfy needs that are not in the best interests of either themselves or their clients.

CLIENTS CALLING THE THERAPIST AT HOME

Many therapists have an unlisted phone number to prevent clients from calling. For those who find an unlisted phone number too troublesome, the problem of calls from clients can be addressed by identifying certain therapeutic ground rules. Many therapists who use written therapeutic contracts have included clear statements that phone calls to the therapist's home will be billed at the same rate as sessions in the office, with the time rounded off to the closest fifteen minutes. This is obviously one way of eliminating some clients from believing they may use the phone for free therapy. Whether the ground rule is established in writing or verbally shared, it is also imperative to communicate that what might be divulged in phone calls may be brought into therapy by the therapist. This rule can prevent calls from clients who hope to use them to share a secret with the therapist in order to create a notion of having something special with the therapist. The sharing of a secret in this fashion can place the therapist in a situation of feeling (and becoming) therapeutically paralyzed.

There are times, regardless of preventive measures, when a client persists in calling. With such clients it is important to address the issue directly in the next face to face session. Therapists should express their concerns about the phone calls directly and in a nonaccusatory fashion while promoting discussion of the implications of frequent calls. The calls may be a manifestation of the client's insecurity and self-perception of not being as competent as the therapist perceives the client to be—and this should be clarified. Another possible reason is that the client is attempting to test the therapist for caring and/or competence; that is, whether the therapist cares enough to talk on the phone, or whether this therapist really means what is said about no home phone calls. Regardless, persistent phone calls should be addressed directly before the therapist gets angry at the client.

TOUCHING CLIENTS

During the course of therapy, there are many times when a particularly emotional exchange has occurred and the therapist may want to express feelings by touch. This type of exchange can often prove valuable and affirming to those involved and promote the therapeutic process, but caution should be exercised.

A male client touched by a male therapist may experience a sense of homosexual panic, or a much more mild sense of uneasiness. Similarly, for a male therapist to touch a female who has been sexually abused, or is otherwise suspicious of others' intentions, could prove detrimental to the therapeutic process. In working with couples, there also exists the possibility that jealousy may be provoked by the therapist's touching one of the spouses, particularly if the therapist has been taking sides during the session with the spouse who is touched. This sort of incident could prove detrimental to what progress has been previously achieved in the couple's therapy.

Therapists should also be sensitive to the widespread publicity that sexual abuse of clients by therapists has received. For instance, a 1986 study of Wisconsin psychologists, family therapists, psychiatrists, social workers, clergy, and other psychotherapists was widely publicized across the country. (Wisconsin Psychological Association, 1987). The results of the survey of 1,559 respondents showed that 310, or 20 percent, had treated clients between 1982 and 1984 who had been involved in a sexual relationship with a previous counselor. The study went on to indicate that 89 percent of the client victims were women and 93 percent of the offending therapists were men. Ninety percent of the respondents to this survey reported believing that the client's welfare had been "seriously and negatively affected by the sexual encounter with his/her therapist." Naturally, such publicity about the therapeutic community is likely to further intensify the potential for misinterpreting an otherwise benign and nobly intended hug or touch on the shoulder.

For reasons such as these, the family therapist is best advised to ask permission prior to hugging a client: for instance, "Right now I am really appreciating the amount of honesty and work you have just demonstrated. Would it be all right if I gave you a hug?" This request serves not only to make the therapist's intentions clear, but also to empower clients and demonstrate to them a respect for the ownership of their bodies and physical boundaries. While being responsive to the divergent backgrounds and perceptions clients bring into our offices, this is also a means of exercising the caution that seems so appropriate today.

SELF-SUPERVISION

After training, the benefit of supervision will not be so available as it was during training. Collegial help can prove valuable as a source of "bouncing ideas around" and deriving benefit, but systems-oriented colleagues may also be unavailable. Although there is truth in the old dictum, "It takes two to know one," meaning that the therapist must receive feedback regarding blind spots, reality dictates that we will not always have others available to us. At these times self-supervision can be helpful in an attempt to examine practices systematically with couples and families.

Frequently, it is helpful to reflect back upon supervised experience received during training in an effort to recall issues that were emphasized with a past supervisor. For instance: "You're attempting to push this family in a direction that reflects your agenda rather than theirs"; "You're being premature in your intervention. You need to do more assessment"; "You're taking too long for assessment and not intervening to effect some change quickly enough"; "You seem to be siding too quickly and too strongly with the adolescent in this family"; or "You seem to be caught up in the content of their presentation to the detriment of understanding their process." Reflecting on frequently uttered statements by past supervisors may disclose areas that are still problematic.

Another option is to periodically or, more particularly, when feeling stuck with a specific case, complete a rating scale/questionnaire such as that provided by Piercy, Laird, and Mohammed (1983). Their rating scale consists of ten items within five broad categories of skills deemed important in the function of family therapy. Reviewing this scale with your own practices in mind can focus attention on areas that may be in need of review and/or identify areas being overlooked that are producing an impasse in working with a particular family.

Professional associations such as the American Association for Marriage and Family Therapy (AAMFT) or the American Family Therapy Association (AFTA) have also begun to establish regional clusters, and these groups provide the benefit of closer contact with like-minded colleagues. It is common for these regional groups to be a rich source of peers who are readily available for support and peer supervision. While the benefit of supervision provided by a skilled supervisor cannot be overstated, the above identified practices can help to offset the absence of supervision.

CLIENTS REJECT/ATTACK ONE COTHERAPIST

This phenomenon will occur at times as a result of simple personality clashes or attempts by the clients to split the cotherapists. A family member may feel attacked by the cotherapy team and choose to react to the cotherapist he or she views as weakest/strongest and most/least vulnerable, or whatever else may govern the choice of target.

At these times it is most valuable for the other cotherapist to remain available to the attacked cotherapist and client as a facilitator to their issue. The available cotherapist can attempt to clarify the concern(s) expressed by the client and ensure that the other cotherapist has effectively heard what was expressed before responding, and so on. In this respect, the available cotherapist can work with the cotherapist-client relationship, much as one would work with spouses who are processing dissonant perceptions of one another, and attempt to achieve some resolution. In this fashion, both cotherapists can effectively model for the couple/family productive means for resolving differences that are probably not characteristic of the family relationships.

Once the session is completed, it is generally valuable for the cotherapists to focus on what occurred and attempt to determine what may have precipitated the attack. This discussion can help them determine what they may have done to contribute to the client's behavior, what its further ramifications may be to the process of therapy, what they can do to avoid attacks in the future, and what should be addressed in the next session. Thus, this is a circumstance that can promote much learning and understanding for the cotherapists rather than simply being an unpleasant incident.

WHEN THERAPIST PROBLEMS INFLUENCE THERAPY

There are obvious times in therapists' lives when it is unlikely they can provide appropriate therapeutic experiences to others. When a therapist is reeling from the death of a loved one, struggling with his or her own divorce, or obsessively consumed with any other life-changing concern, the intrapersonal interference will likely be too great to facilitate effective therapy. Therapists can conduct an internal inventory to determine when issues of this nature are so dramatically present that it would be best to postpone scheduled sessions. At these times the difficulty in concentrating on the clients' concerns is usually self-evident.

There are also more subtle therapist difficulties that may prove counterproductive to therapy. Adequate assessment of these problems requires the use of a consultant. We can often benefit from the feedback of another person to help us more clearly perceive our blind spots. For example, a therapist consistently sides with the parents against their adolescent son, which predictably leads the son to escalate his acting out. This escalating pattern may occur for several sessions, until the therapist gets a consultant who helps to clarify how the therapist is fighting the therapist's own adolescent son through a client family's struggle. With this new awareness the therapist can become more judicious in joining both parents and adolescent; without this awareness, the therapist will continue to be a factor that not only promotes maintenance, but intensifies the pattern the family presents. At such times the consultant may be a colleague, spouse, or some other person who is capable of providing the necessary perspective from outside the therapist's circumscribed self-perceptions.

When therapists find themselves stuck with a particular case and/or are receiving consistent feedback expressing concerns from a family, a consult will also likely prove valuable. Perhaps the therapist is simply overlooking an obvious piece of the family's operation that needs attention, but the therapist may also have become blinded by his or her own intrapersonally motivated distortions. Many therapists have found an ongoing professional support group invaluable in this regard. The fact that the group is an ongoing effort facilitates the members' coming to know one another well enough that valuable case consultation can be provided in regard to these difficult situations. If this type of problem recurs, the therapist might find it beneficial to consider entering therapy to determine the source of repeated distortions or blocks.

≡≡≡7 ≡ ADJUNCTIVE PROCEDURES

INTRODUCTION

Adjunctive procedures, as a group, are more than a mere collection of procedures that do not fit neatly into the categories discussed in preceding chapters. All professionals confront unusual problems and issues in practice. Family therapists are no different and likewise need to know what to do in such circumstances. For example, what does a therapist do if a member of a client family is handicapped? Under what conditions is bibliotherapy appropriate or when can letters be most helpful to clients? How can a family member who is important to the therapy or a particular session but lives far away become constructively involved? In these situations a single procedure is not sufficient and a style of therapy somewhat different from the usual is needed.

BIBLIOTHERAPY

The use of reading material as part of the therapeutic process, or bibliotherapy, can be a valuable therapeutic adjunct that expands the impact of a single session. Using assigned reading material to prepare clients for a session or as a follow-up to what transpired in session can significantly increase the efficacy and impact of therapy.

Areas of focus for which bibliotherapy is applicable include parent-child interactions, interpersonal communications, and family activities; it can also enhance cognitive understanding of phenomena such as depression. More recently, an impressive and helpful body of literature appropriate for use with the lay public has evolved around the issue of being the adult child of an alcoholic. These resources can help individuals, and couples, in the process of developing a new understanding of the behavior that has proven troublesome to them, and this understanding could provide a valuable springboard to effecting change. Books such as the following are particularly helpful in this regard: *It Will Never Happen to Me* (Black, 1981), *Children of Alcoholics* (Ackerman, 1983), *Guide to Recovery: A Book for Adult Children of Alcoholics* (Gravitz & Bowden, 1985), and *Adult Children of Alcoholics* (Woititz, 1983).

An important issue in utilizing bibliotherapy is the makeup of the client for whom the reading is intended. Those clients who have had unpleasant school experiences and who do not read extensively should not be encouraged to read a large, hardcover book with small print. Such a book will probably not be read, and the client will feel embarrassed about returning for the next session and/or angry at the therapist's apparent lack of sensitivity to the client as an individual. The books identified above are all paperbacks, and they are very concrete and practical in style. Typically, a paperback book is less intimidating to the reader and is more likely to be read.

A frequently used bibliotherapeutic aid is *Single Parenting: A Practical Resource Guide* (Atlas, 1981). It is a paperback and—true to its title—practical in its orientation and the ideas provided. Although it is not a "how to" book, Thurber's story "The Secret Life of Walter Mitty" is a good resource to illustrate how one can indulge in fantasies to the extent that life passes by without being recognized for what it is, or could be.

A derivative of this approach is that discussed by Hamburg (1983). He discusses how he frequently has couples read aloud, alternating reading time, *The Intimate Enemy: How to Fight Fair in Love and Marriage* (Bach & Wyden, 1970). He has found the experience to have immediate "face validity" to distressed couples, helping them to understand their damaging conflict styles. The book universalizes and normalizes their difficulties and introduces them to new options for conflict resolution. He maintains that reading aloud encourages them to engage in a cooperative endeavor that is not patronizing, but that directly addresses the concern they present while stimulating cooperative behavior.

As with other assignments, it is crucial for the therapist to check with the clients to determine their reaction to suggested reading. If the reading is suggested and then never followed up, the client may conclude that the therapist throws out ideas with little regard. Also, the greatest benefit from bibliotherapy stems from its integration into the therapy and the clients' lives, which will involve some discussion to promote application.

THERAPY WITH A HANDICAPPED FAMILY MEMBER

Families will often be seen wherein one member has a particular disease or anomaly that may not be the primary presenting problem, but does constitute a chronic stressor that depletes the family's resources. Examples include Alzheimer's disease, cerebral palsy, mental retardation, diabetes, learning disabilities, cancer, heart disease, and brain disorders. Although therapy may help the family to organize and realign itself in ways that lessen the impact of these problems on their functioning, the wise therapist will also be alert to the many community resources that are developing to assist with these types of matters. For instance, many departments of social welfare have developed programs that make available respite care opportunities to those families with a disabled member. These services can provide families with assistance that allows them to take long-postponed vacations or periodic breaks. Also, many communities today have support groups available to members of families with someone who has a learning disability, cancer, retardation, heart disease, or other such condition. These groups, populated by others in similar circumstances, can provide valuable education and support that cannot be offered in the same way by family therapists. Perhaps Al-Anon and Alateen—the services provided to spouses and children of alcoholics, respectively—have best demonstrated over the years the value of community-based support groups to family members. This type of referral and subsequent involvement can often prove therapeutic by involving family members in the community outside of their obsession with themselves and their family. Certainly, most who have lived in a family with a member with a chronic disorder can understand how this sort of problem can exacerbate other problems of family living.

The availability of these types of services can usually be determined by contacting the local chamber of commerce or the director of the area social services department. Learning the name of a contact person in each of these groups to facilitate the referral process can prove to be the most therapeutic activity a family therapist can perform.

THERAPY WITH A MENTALLY ILL FAMILY MEMBER

Occasionally, a family will be seen with a member who has been diagnosed as having one of the major affective disorders or schizophrenias and is being treated by a psychiatrist. In these situations it becomes imperative to develop an understanding and, one hopes, a therapeutic alliance with the attending psychiatrist. To do otherwise, and particularly to do battle with the psychiatrist, can prove counterproductive to the family and the diagnosed family member, not to mention the energy and reputation of the family therapist. For example, psychiatrists have frequently used psychotropic medications to treat various mental conditions, and these have proven highly successful in resolving troublesome symptoms. The family therapist who is too quick to encourage a family member to stop taking prescribed medications "because your mental illness is only a reflection or metaphor for what's happening in this family" could run the risk of a territorial battle with the medical profession and possible lawsuits for malpractice or negligence. Just as a diagnosed mental illness can serve to mask major family problems as the family becomes consumed with the illness, a battle between therapist and psychiatrist could serve to distract the family and provide them with other "hiding places" that postpone or prevent the most effective treatment from being delivered.

While family therapy is partly rooted in work with schizophrenics and attempts to describe the mental illness as being reactive to, and a metaphor for, the family process, psychotropic medications are now widely accepted and successful in addressing many of the major distressing symptoms observed. For these reasons the therapist is well advised to develop a cooperative relationship with the attending psychiatrist that will enhance the potential value of family therapy. Naturally, trying to convince psychiatrists of the potential negative ramifications of their medications is unlikely to foster this type of cooperative relationship. It is more important and valuable to enlist the psychiatrist as the valuable member of the treatment team that he or she can be. Without understanding your treatment plan and receiving input regarding progress and interactions observed in the family sessions, psychiatrists will not be nearly so able to respond to their patients in the most effective manner. With the benefit of a cooperative relationship, attending psychiatrists are typically very responsive to suggestions that are offered. As might be expected, while some are very aware of principles of family therapy, most psychiatrists are more keenly aware of medications as their special treatment modality; thus, cooperation of the family therapist and psychiatrist can promote a definite synergistic effect for the patient and family.

David Keith, a psychiatrist also well known for his family therapy skills, has noted the following regarding the use of lithium in the treatment of manic-depressive illness: "Lithium is helpful and should be used, but it does not define the parameters of the family struggle" (1980, p.53). While Keith's article focuses on how medication, particularly lithium, may be viewed as the panacea to all of the tensions present in the family, there is also present the recognition of the value medications can have in facilitating family therapy and what is in the best interest of the diagnosed person.

THERAPY WITH COURT-REFERRED CLIENTS

Many therapists have mixed feelings about working with court-referred clients. Whether the court refers for chemical abuse evaluation, incest, or family violence treatment, such clients typically have many problems (for example, low income and minimal education) that are not amenable to therapy treatment alone. The problems that are amenable to treatment tend to be those in the category of more severe pathology. In addition, chronic offenders who are sentenced to treatment typically have had a good deal of experience with social workers, psychiatrists, psychologists, and other mental health professionals who are perceived as allies of the court and not to be trusted. Family therapists may be seen as more threatening than individually oriented helping agents because the therapy will invade the offender's intimate interpersonal life and involve persons who may have a great deal of power. All of these issues compound the usual difficulties encountered in therapy.

The training therapists receive is also a hindrance. Most clients seen by therapists in training are those who have sought therapy. Consequently, the therapist has no power to exercise other than that produced through displays of competence and interpersonal skill. The therapist of a court-referred client, however, can exercise real coercive power. Since therapists are not trained to use this power and are socialized not to coerce clients, the tools provided by the courts often are ignored.

In working with court-referred clients, clinicians have been most successful when they have clarified their role at the outset. Role clarification consists of first conferring with the county attorney or other legal officer to determine the therapist's responsibilities. Most often the referral of a perpetrator to therapy means that instead of jail, the perpetrator will attend sessions and cooperate. Referral to a family therapist implies that the perpetrator's family must do likewise. The only way to find out who must attend sessions and for how long is to ask the supervising attorney.

The therapist's role must also be clarified with the clients in the initial session. With clients who are in trouble for the first time, it is helpful to state that the therapist is not a police officer or their parole officer. Commonly, reports of the client's progress will be asked for by the court, and the client should be made aware of that fact. Even so, the therapist can differentiate himself or herself from the authorities by stating that family therapy is designed to help the family function better, not to analyze the family for faults or to serve as an alternate punishment. When the client can differentiate between therapy and punishment, therapy can proceed as with a typical client family.

For the vast majority of court-referred clients, however, the therapist needs the power granted by the courts, and the client needs to know that he or she will remain in therapy and perhaps out of jail only as long as therapy progresses satisfactorily. The therapist does not attempt to establish difference from the authorities, but instead joins with them to work on improving family functioning. The client is told that regular attendance at sessions and cooperation by family members is expected. If sessions are missed or if the client refuses to cooperate, therapy will terminate and a report detailing the client's behavior will be sent to the supervising officer. After this discussion, therapy can begin with a discussion of what family therapy is about and a statement of the goals of family therapy before the actual treatment process commences.

LETTERS TO CLIENTS AS THERAPY

There are times when use of letters can constitute a significant part of therapy. Letters are appropriate when used (1) to express appreciation and caring beyond the usual in-session means, (2) to send a message that the therapist wants to assure is "received," (3) to ensure a time of family togetherness with a focus on a particular topic, or (4) to share a forgotten assignment or the therapist's afterthoughts to a session.

In the busy schedule of most therapists there are times when appreciation or caring for particular clients is not voiced. For instance, while doing an intake with a family, the therapist is reminded of another family that had a similar initial presentation and has now progressed considerably. That reminiscence also reminds the therapist that he or she has not provided them with the affirmation they are due. At this time an unexpected letter of affirmation to that family can prove very therapeutic as they collectively share the affirmation and acknowledgment of their accomplishments. Therapists can take their clients for granted as easily as family members can do with one another.

Putting a message in writing can also serve to accent its importance and improve the chances of its being received. For instance, there may be a time when the therapist desires to prescribe the symptom presented by the family, or the therapist may think that a prescription for a piece of particularly troublesome family interaction could benefit from being placed in writing and sent to the family with the directive that they all read it at least once and then discuss its implications before the next session.

Letters can also be used as a means of directly intervening with the family. For instance, the family may be told to expect a letter from the therapist and to be prepared to engage in what the letter requests. This creates an air of anticipation and excitement that better ensures completion of the assignment than does having the same message uttered at the end of a session. For example, a letter may be sent asking the family to identify a thirty-minute period within three days of its receipt to be used by each family member to identify two things they believe they could do to help the family situation. The outcome of this assignment can then be dealt with in the next session.

When the therapist simply forgets to make an assignment or issue a request of the family, a letter can prove helpful. Rather than waiting for the next session, and possibly losing time, a short handwritten note can serve to cover for the oversight and better capitalize on the time available in session. This type of letter also seems to have the effect of providing the family with another means of feeling affirmed by the therapist, as they realize they are in the therapist's thoughts beyond the time they are together.

THERAPY WITH CULTURALLY DISTINCT FAMILIES

A number of authors—McGoldrick, Pearce, and Giordano (1982) being the best known—have written about the implications of culture on family therapy and the need to tailor therapy to the needs of families from cultures different from that of the therapist. Their position is that culture makes a difference and that if therapy is to be successful, it must be carried out in a manner that is consonant with cultural values and heritage.

Therapy is benefited if the therapist has experience living in the clients' culture, whether they come from another nation or another neighborhood. Without the shared meaning of symbols produced by this living experience, errors and misunderstandings are inevitable. But the simple misunderstanding of verbal and nonverbal messages is not the major problem in working with culturally different families. If it were, only a multilanguage dictionary would be needed in every consulting room.

Different power and role structures are also not principal issues that influence therapy with culturally different families. A variety of family structures is present within any culture. In fact, the range of family role and power structures within cultures is probably as great as that between cultures. Besides the obvious problem of mutual understanding of language, the principal difficulty for a therapist whose clients are from a different culture lies in correctly interpreting the metaphorical implications of symptoms and in pacing therapy according to the interpersonal norms of the family.

Regarding the latter, for example, families with strong multigenerational ties and allegiances may need more session time allocated to trust-building before the members risk disclosing the problems they experience. Among cultures where the male role is authoritarian, family violence may be described obliquely, and the therapist must be sensitive to language nuances to pick up what is being disclosed. Where the status and role differences between men and women are large, confronting the family homeostasis by interviewing the wife alone during the initial phase of therapy may prompt the family to terminate. In general, avoiding mistakes when working with families from different cultures requires knowing a good deal about how people conduct themselves and their family life.

While it is important to consider cultural differences in conducting therapy, it is more important to recognize that the basic processes governing family life and individual behavior are the same regardless of the socioeconomic status or cultural heritage of a family. The ramification of believing otherwise is enormous because the foundation of family therapy is family theory, and especially family system theory, which by definition must apply to all families no matter what their heritage or lifestyle. Attaching too much significance to cultural differences whether in diagnosis or treatment is to abandon the benefits of family system therapy and to retreat to a less sophisticated and less effective style of intervention.

≡≡8≡ IMPLICATIONS FOR RESEARCH

As a discipline, family therapy has only recently begun to bridge a long-standing split between researchers and therapists. A conference held at the Eastern Pennsylvania Psychiatric Institute in 1967 was designed to stimulate a dialogue between the parties. The level of the issues discussed is evident from the four basic research questions posed at the conference by Jay Haley (1972):

1. Is there a difference between families with a psychiatrically abnormal member and families with normal members?
2. Do families differ according to the type of abnormality present in the disturbed member?
3. Is one part of a family different from another part?
4. Do family systems change after successful therapy?

Presently, definitive answers to the first three of these questions have not been delivered by either therapists or researchers. Part of the problem certainly lies in the complexity of the family, but also pertinent is the lack of research training among family therapists. Few doctoral programs are currently offered, and only recently has the American Association for Marriage and Family Therapy (AAMFT) formulated standards for doctoral training in family therapy. In addition, the field has not adopted a scientist-practitioner model for its members. As a result, the practice side of the field has developed without an adequate empirical foundation (Gurman, 1983).

Given these impediments, it is unlikely that enough research attention will be brought to bear on answering the important questions in the near term. An alternative to focusing on these more basic family science questions is to focus the energy of practitioners on therapy and the procedures that make it up. As a result of learning what does and does not work and why, knowledge of the way families function and answers to all of Jay Haley's questions may be expedited.

Except for the communication skills teaching methods, none of the procedures described in this book have been empirically validated. That is not to say they do not work; experience has taught us that they do. But assessments of procedural reliability across clients, family systems, presenting problems, and therapists have not been conducted. Consequently, each procedure described in this text can stimulate a human interaction study that can draw on social exchange theory or a host of other interpersonal theories for hypothesis testing.

Take, for example, the procedure on ending chitchat described in Chapter 4. The procedure consists of using a directive/transition statement to communicate to clients that chitchat has ended and the session is beginning. The research question used to guide the study of this procedure might be "What is the relationship between directive/transition statements made by a therapist at the beginning of a session and continued small talk by clients?" The research design might consist of recording the duration of small talk by clients when a therapist uses directive/transition statements and when no such statement is used to mark the beginning of a session. The findings would either support continued use of the procedure, suggest another procedure should be created, or indicate that clients do not need prompting to begin sessions. In any case, the attention of researchers would be focused on the pattern of interaction among the participants in therapy. We would certainly learn more about the process of therapy. As a result, we may come one small step closer to answering the questions about families that were posed by Jay Haley.

Some may argue that this approach to family research will yield a mass of information that is as worthless as that produced by the psychotherapy process research that was popular in the 1940s through the 1960s. Many reviewers have stated that while the goals of that research were noble, the products were of marginal value (Auld & Murray, 1955; Cartwright, 1957; Dittes, 1959; Kiesler, 1973; Marsden, 1971; Strupp, 1962). The most often stated reason for this seeming failure is that most researchers did not carry out long-term research programs. Instead, they indulged in bursts of idiosyncratic interest in a single variable (Truax & Carkhuff, 1967). Large-scale chaos with minimal attempts to integrate and replicate methods and findings was the result (Kiesler, 1973).

To avoid the same outcome, family therapy process research of the type called for here will require consideration of the many methodological issues presented by Kiesler (1973). First, he argues that the process investigator must have a clear conceptualization of the construct or constructs that are measured. For example, social exchange theory might be used to examine the exchange of short-term verbal rewards in an initial session and to predict the likelihood of clients' returning for a second session or to predict client behavior during the initial session. Process research in the past has not conformed to the scientific method. As a result, concepts were not accurately translated into variables, and, in turn, appropriate data were not collected to test hypotheses. The findings of research on family therapy procedures must have implications for some theory if the findings are to be valued and integrated into a body of credible research that impacts on the practice of therapy.

Once the variables under study have been defined, the investigator must decide on a unit of analysis, which will typically be therapist and/or client behavior or some "chunk" of interaction that will be counted or rated in some way. The unit of analysis chosen will depend on the construct(s) of interest. For example, to study the impact of relationship development procedures on the likelihood that clients will agree with a reframe of their presenting symptoms, the joining behavior of a therapist—expressions of empathy, for instance—might be measured. The unit of analysis in measuring empathy includes not just the therapist's verbal statement, but also the client's remark before the therapist's empathic statement, as well as the client's response afterwards. Selecting an appropriate unit of analysis requires preliminary testing of different units and the willingness to examine interaction in detail before the study is carried out.

Another issue requiring a decision is sampling. Findings that can be generalized beyond a particular case or instance within a particular session are interesting but of limited value in evaluating practice procedures. Since it is usually impractical to collect and analyze the data from a whole therapy session or case, sampling must be employed. As pointed out by Kiesler (1973), sampling must be considered within the theoretical concepts being studied. To continue with the example cited above, since relationship development and the reframing of symptoms typically occur earlier rather than later in therapy, sampling the first three sessions of many cases would be more appropriate than sampling all the sessions of a few cases.

Beyond deciding the units of analysis and the sampling method, the nuts and bolts of collecting and scoring the data must be considered. Whether process research involves qualitative or quantitative variables, it demands the use of highly reliable methods of rating interactions. Judges and raters must be highly trained, and their reliability must be tested and retested throughout a study. As a result of making these decisions, the researcher will be pleasantly surprised not only by the findings but also by the depth of understanding about therapy and the functioning of families developed by the exercise of research. Consequently, therapists who tackle the study of the therapeutic process can and will provide answers to the important questions.

If the field were to examine its procedure in a systematic manner, several outcomes would be apparent. Most importantly, our profession needs to grow toward more rigor. We have enough vigor, as is obvious by the number of new titles published each year, but a more sound basis for practice is needed to support continued public confidence in consuming family therapy services. It will not be long before legislators and the insurance industry demand that the benefits of psychotherapy services be directly traceable to the procedures used by clinicians. Without establishing such validity, we risk loss of not only our status as a profession but our livelihood as well.

Another important research issue involves clinical use of research findings published in the journals. While all MFT graduate programs include course work in research methods and many students conduct theses as part of their program requirements, the integration of research into practice is not easy. For example, a review study on the overall effectiveness of the MFT, such as has been conducted by Gurman and Kniskern (1978), may bolster the confidence of a clinician and provide very broad guidelines for treatment but offer little help for the next therapy session. We are rapidly approaching the time when research will address issues and questions that have direct application in therapy. Meanwhile, the question remains: "How can a clinician best use the research that is being conducted today?"

The prerequisite to using the research is knowing that it exists. Nearly all of our professional associations publish journals that contain scholarly and research contributions. Reading the journals from cover to cover is the best way to become aware of what might be useful. It is tempting to skim the contents page of a particular journal issue and then read only those articles of interest. To get the full benefit of the dues paid for membership in professional organizations, however, therapists need to read journals thoroughly and on a regular basis. Good clinicians make journal reading a regular habit.

Most journal editors and their review boards do an excellent job of screening what they publish, and the reader can trust that several leaders in the field have examined published articles for major flaws and inaccuracies. The scholarly article, wherein an author presents an issue and then a supporting argument, is evaluated based on the validity of the argument(s). Research articles are more difficult for the average reader to evaluate because the intricacies of research design and statistical analysis require advanced training to know whether the findings are trustworthy. Here again, the journal editor's task is to make sure that accepted design and statistical procedures were used and that the author's conclusions were not exaggerated or incorrect. Even with this safeguard, the reader must remain cautious.

Consider a study that is designed to find out why clients do not return for therapy after an initial session. In attempting to answer the question, the investigator interviewed many but not all nonreturning clients from a local clinic over a two-month period and asked them why they did not stay in therapy. The reasons listed by clients were collated, and the five most frequently stated reasons were reported. In the discussion section of the article, the author concluded that even with the limitations of the study, the improvement of return rates was dependent on a clinician's making sure to avoid certain mistakes.

Clearly, the rate of client return after the initial session is an important one, especially for private practitioners. If the reader merely reads the abstract and the discussion section of the article, and then implements changes in his or her practice, the results may or may not meet expectations. The flaws in this study of course are that not all nonreturning clients were interviewed and the clientele of the clinic in the study may be different from that of the reader's. The results, while interesting, may not apply to all clinical settings. In addition, the study was designed to find out why clients do not return after an initial session, not what works to keep clients in therapy—a related but different question.

The value of the study for the clinician, however, lies not merely in the findings but in the framing of the question and the method used to answer it. If the reader has a similar problem in his or her practice, the procedure described in the article can be tailored to the reader's situation to determine why clients are not returning, and changes can then be instituted where appropriate.

Besides learning how to improve one's practice, a second and very important use of research for clinicians is in building a full knowledge of the field of family therapy. Early in a clinician's career, the developmental task consists of learning the basics of professional practice. With experience, competence grows and a sense of mastery develops. Full mastery is never attained, of course, but part of becoming an accomplished clinician and avoiding burnout consists of expanding one's grasp of the field in all of its aspects. Reading not only the newest ideas but also the research, which is nearly always years behind in testing those ideas, is the most convenient way to keep up with and to develop a broader view of the field. As a result of maintaining a fieldwide view of family therapy through reading the research, the clinician is given the opportunity to take ownership of his or her profession.

In large part, increasing ownership of the marriage and family therapy profession has been the goal of this book. We claim that procedure exists in the practice of marriage and family therapy. In doing so, we reject the notion that family therapy is a mere group of connected ideas easily adapted to any sort of mental health practice. There is a way to go about the effective practice of family therapy. We also know that the procedures stated here need systematic evaluation beyond that conducted by ourselves. Nonetheless, we are confident that if learned and implemented, these procedures represent a good starting point for the beginning clinician to take ownership of the profession.

REFERENCES

Ackerman, N. W. (1958). Toward an integrative therapy of the family. *American Journal of Psychiatry, 8*, 727–733.

Ackerman, R. J. (1983). *Children of alcoholics*. Holmes Beach, FL: Learning Publications.

Anderson, C. M., & Stewart, S. (1983). *Mastering resistance: A practical guide to family therapy.* New York: The Guilford Press.

Atlas, S. L. (1981). *Single parenting: A practical resource guide*. Englewood Cliffs, NJ: Prentice-Hall.

Auld, F., & Murray, E. (1955). Content-analysis studies of psychotherapy. *Psychological Bulletin, 52*, 377–395.

Bach, G., & Wyden, P. (1970). *The intimate enemy: How to fight fair in love and marriage*. New York: William Morrow & Co.

Barnard, C. P., & Corrales, R. G. (1979). *The theory and technique of family therapy.* Springfield, IL: Charles C. Thomas.

Black, C. (1981). *It will never happen to me*. Denver, CO: M.A.C.

Bossard, J., & Boll, E. (1950). *Ritual in family living*. Philadelphia: University of Pennsylvania Press.

Boszormenyi-Nagy, I., & Spark, G. (1973). *Invisible loyalties*. New York: Harper & Row.

Bowen, M. (1976). Theory in the practice of psychotherapy. In P. J. Guerin (Ed.), *Family therapy: Theory and practice* (pp. 43–90). New York: Gardner Press.

Brock, G., & Sanderson, B. (1984). Social exchange in the initial family therapy interview. *Journal of Marital and Family Therapy, 10*, 317–320.

Cartwright, D. S. (1957). Annotated bibliography of research and theory construction in client centered therapy. *Journal of Counseling Psychology, 4*, 82–100.

Cartwright, D. (1966). Analysis of qualitative material. In L. Festinger & D. Katz (Eds.), *Research methods in the behavioral sciences* (pp. 421–470). New York: Holt, Reinhart & Winston.

de Shazer, S. (1982). *Patterns of brief family therapy.* New York: The Guilford Press.

Dittes, J. (1959). Previous studies bearing on content analysis of psychotherapy. In J. Dollard & F. Auld (Eds.), *Scoring human motives: A manual* (pp. 325–351). New Haven, CT: Yale University Press.

Finkelhor, D. (1979). *Sexually victimized children.* New York: Free Press.

Granvold, D. K., & Tarrant, R. (1983). Structured marital separation as a marital treatment method. *Journal of Marital and Family Therapy, 9,* 189–198.

Gravitz, H. L., & Bowden, J. D. (1985). *Guide to recovery: A book for adult children of alcoholics.* Holmes Beach, FL: Learning Publications.

Gurman, A. (1983). Family therapy research and the "new epistemology." *Journal of Marital and Family Therapy, 9,* 227–234.

Gurman, A., & Kniskern, D. (1978). Research on marital and family therapy: Progress, perspective and prospect. In S. Garfield & A. Bergin (Eds.), *Handbook of psychotherapy and behavior change* (2nd ed.) New York: Wiley.

Haley, J. (1972). Critical overview of present status of family interaction research. In J. Framo (Ed.), *Family interaction: A dialogue between family researchers and family therapists.* New York: Springer.

Haley, J. (1973). *Uncommon therapy.* New York: Ballantine.

Haley, J. (1976). *Problem solving therapy.* San Francisco, CA: Jossey-Bass.

Hamburg, S. R. (1983). Reading aloud as an initial assignment in marital therapy. *Journal of Marital and Family Therapy, 9,* 81–88.

Hill, R. (1958). Generic features of families under stress. *Social Casework, 49,* 139–150.

Hoffman, L. (1976). Breaking the homeostatic cycle, In P. J. Guerin (Ed.), *Family Therapy: Theory and Practice.* (pp. 501–519). New York: Gardner Press.

Holmes, T. H., & Rahe, R. (1967). The social readjustment rating scale. *Journal of Psychosomatic Research, 11,* 213–218.

Johnson, V. E. (1973). *I'll quit tomorrow.* New York: Harper & Row.

Keith, D. V. (1980). Family therapy and lithium deficiency. *Journal of Marital and Family Therapy, 6,* 49–54.

Kiesler, D. (1973). *The process of psychotherapy.* Chicago: Aldine.

Lewis, J. M., Beavers, W. R., Gossett, J. T., & Phillips, V. A. (1976). *No single thread: psychological health in family systems.* New York: Brunner/Mazel.

Marsden, G. (1971). Content-analysis studies of psychotherapy: 1954 through 1968. In A. Bergin & S. Garfield (Eds.), *Handbook of psychotherapy and behavior change* (pp. 345–407). New York: Wiley.

MacAndrew, C. (1965). The differentiation of male alcoholic outpatients from non-alcoholic psychiatric patients by means of the MMPI. *Quarterly Journal of Studies on Alcohol, 26,* 238–246.

McCubbin, H. I., & Patterson, J. M. (1982). Family adaptation to crises. In H. McCubbin, A. Cauble, & J. Patterson (Eds.), *Family stress, coping and social support.* Springfield, IL: Charles C. Thomas.

McGoldrick, M., Pearce, J. & Giordano, J. (1982). *Ethnicity and family therapy.* New York: The Guilford Press.

Meisel, P., & Kendrick, W., (1985). *Bloomsbury/Freud.* New York: Basic Books.

Minuchin, S. (1974). *Families and family therapy.* Cambridge, MA: Harvard University Press.

Minuchin, S., and Fishman, H. C. (1981). *Family therapy techniques.* Cambridge: Harvard University Press.

Napier, A., & Whitaker, C. A. (1978). *The family crucible*. New York: Harper & Row.

Navran, L. (1973). *Marital diagnostic inventory.* Los Angeles: Western Psychological Services.

O'Brian, C., & Bruggen, P. (1985). Our personal and professional lives: Learning positive connotation and circular questioning. *Family Process, 24*, 311–322.

Oliveri, M., & Reiss, D. (1982). Family styles of construing the social environment: A perspective on variation among nonclinical families. In F. Walsh (Ed.), *Normal family processes* (pp. 94–114). New York: The Guilford Press.

Olson, D. H., & McCubbin, H. I. (1982). Circumplex model of marital and family systems V: Application to family stress and crises intervention. In H. I. McCubbin, A. Cauble, & J. Patterson (Eds.), *Family stress, coping and social support*. Springfield, IL: Charles C. Thomas.

Palazzoli-Selvini, M., Boscolo, L., GianFranco, C., & Prata, G. (1980). The problem of the referring person. *Journal of Marital and Family Therapy, 6*, 3–10.

Paul, N. (1967). The use of empathy in the resolution of grief. *Perspectives in Biology and Medicine, 11*, 153–169.

Piercy, F. P., Laird, R. A., & Mohammed, Z. (1983). A family therapist rating scale. *Journal of Marital and Family Therapy, 9*, 49–60.

Reddy, B. (1973). *Alcoholism: A family illness*. Park Ridge, IL: Lutheran General Hospital.

Richman, J. (1986). *Family therapy for suicidal people*. New York: Springer.

Rogers, C. (1951). *Client centered therapy.* Boston: Houghton Mifflin.

Schvaneveldt, J., & Lee, T. (1983). The emergence and practice of ritual in the American family. *Family Perspective, 17*, 137–143.

Selzer, M. L. (1971). The Michigan alcoholism screening test: The quest for a new diagnostic instrument. *American Journal of Psychiatry, 127*, 1653–1658.

Smets, A. (1985). Personal communication.

Stahmann, R., & Heibert, W. (1977). The initial interview. In R. Stahmann & W. Heibert (Eds.), *Klemer's counseling in marital and sexual problems* (2nd ed.) (pp. 34–49). Baltimore: Williams & Wilkins.

Stanton, M., Todd, T., & Associates (1982). *The family therapy of drug abuse and addiction*. New York: The Guilford Press.

Straus, M. A. (1978). Wife beating: How common and why? *Victimology, 2*, 443–458.

Straus, M. A., & Brown, B. W. (1978). *Family measurement techniques*. Minneapolis: University of Minnesota Press.

Strupp, H. (1962). Patient-doctor relationships in the therapeutic process. In A. Bachrach (Ed.), *Experimental foundations of clinical psychology* (pp. 576–615). New York: Basic Books.

Truax, C., & Carkhuff, R. (1967). *Toward effective counseling and psychotherapy.* Chicago: Aldine.

Walker, L. (1978). The development, implementation, and evaluation of two educational models of family intervention (Doctoral dissertation, the University of Texas at Austin, 1978). *Dissertation Abstracts International, 39*, 2160A.

Walker, L. E. (1979). *The battered woman*. New York: Harper & Row.

Walsh, F. (1982). *Normal family processes*. New York: The Guilford Press.

Watzlawick, P., Weakland, J. H., & Fisch, R. (1974). *Change: Principles of problem formation and problem resolution.* New York: Norton.

Weber, T., McKeever, J., & McDaniel, S. (1985). A beginner's guide to the problem oriented first family interview. *Family Process, 24,* 357–364.

Wegscheider, S. (1981). *Another chance: Hope and health for the alcoholic family.* Palo Alto, CA: Science & Behavior Books.

Weitzman, J., & Dreen, K. (1982). Wifebeating: A view of the marital dyad. *Social Casework, 63,* 259–265.

Wisconsin Psychological Association (1987). *Survey of Sexual Misconduct by Psychotherapists and Counselors.* Madison, WI.

Woititz, J. G. (1983). *Adult children of alcoholics.* Hollywood, FL: Health Communications.

Wolin, Bennett, Noonan, & Teitelbaum, (1980). Disrupted family rituals: A factor in the intergenerational transmission of alcoholism. *Journal of Studies on Alcohol, 41,* 199–213.

Zuk, G. H. (1981). *Family therapy: A triadic-based approach.* New York: Human Sciences Press.

AUTHOR INDEX

SUBJECT INDEX